Lead, Achieve, and Succeed in HR

Pamela J. Green, SPHR

WESTCOM PRESS

New York   Los Angeles   Washington DC

Westcom Press
2101 N Street, NW
Suite T-1
Washington, DC 20037

westcomassociates@mac.com

18 17 16 15 14 13 12 11 1 2 3 4 5

ISBN: 978-0-9835003-3-9

Success is not the result of spontaneous combustion. You must set yourself on fire.

—Reggie Leach

This book is dedicated to my mother and father.
Thanks for the match.

Contents

Opening Words

When I started writing this book several years ago, my mind had pictures of a much different end product. At that time, Twitter wasn't around, Facebook and LinkedIn were a blip on the screen, and the economy was good. Though we were at war, employees stood around the water cooler talking about American Idol and the latest episode of Alias. Networking was a local thing, and globalization wasn't something to really concern yourself with, especially not in HR. Everyone wanted to be like Southwest Airlines, and we were reading the books Contented Cows Get More Milk and 1001 Ways to Reward Employees. Words like "normalization," "balanced scorecard," and Sarbanes Oxley filled our lips and our minds. Tom Brokaw, Peter Jennings, and Dan Rather were still the ones we primarily turned to for news and information in a tightly woven 30-minute sound bite. When someone mentioned a tea party, they weren't talking about politics. We were just starting to talk more about having "a seat at the table." We worried about the retiring Baby Boomers. We were deciding on whether to pursue an MBA or MLHR graduate degree. We still felt a sense of responsibility for helping employees manage their careers. For the most part, HR was staying in its lane and doing pretty well staying out of the fray of the media spotlight. So life was different when I started writing this book. Had I finished this book back then, it would've been a checklist for maintaining a relatively good and stable career in HR.

Lots of things happened between then and now. HR is talking about ROI, ROE, B2B, and MNE's. We have a strong presence on Twitter and HR groups on LinkedIn. Companies have landing pages on Facebook, and if you haven't snagged your name as a URL, well, you've been left behind. Networking is global, and HR professionals are trying to focus on their strategic contribution to the organization as opposed to a seat at the table. At the water cooler, we're still talking about American Idol, but we've added The Apprentice and cable news programs. We're trying to decide whether to get an MBA or a JD. We're building competency in finance, marketing, communication, and globalization. The customer is no longer just internal— we've got our eye on the needs of the external customer as well and we've got our dial tuned to what is keeping our CEO up at night. Since Baby Boomers can't retire because of the economy, young professionals, human capital, external influences, globalization, HR Innovation, scenario plans, employee engagement, workforce planning, ethics, sustainability, and business model are the buzz words and hot topics of the day for HR. Did I mention that everyone is branding themselves?

Two totally different books indeed, but one thing remains constant: while we're keeping up with everything and everyone else, we're still struggling with our own development. Many will read the paragraph above, and while some will say, "Yeah, that sounds about right," others will say, "I'm not doing that" and "Who has time for all of that?" Well, the world of HR will continue to change, and only those who can keep up and change with the world around them will survive. Who knows, by the time this book is published, maybe we'll have gone from the Human Resources Department to the Human Capital Department or something else. The point is we must keep up with the demands of the changing world of work. HR is no longer just about HR. We have to broaden our scope to keep up with these and many other changes. Just as an athlete conditions for a game, human resource professionals have to stay in top condition to remain relevant, credible, and resourceful leaders for the current and future workforce. Are you keeping up?

T or **F** You know who your company's business and talent competitors are and are implementing, working under, or have executed and communicated a talent strategy.

T or **F** You are at the same skill level (or higher) as newly hired professionals in your job group.

T or **F** You feel you are keeping up with business demands and any changes to your HR role.

T or **F** Annually you participate in at least 20 hours of training and development that help you stay abreast of changes in business and human resources.

T or **F** HR is a career you can see yourself retiring from.

T or **F** You have developed yourself such that should you get laid off, you are confident that you could quickly find another position in human resources.

T or **F** You have written and follow a plan for your career.

T or **F** If surveyed, co-workers, peers, leaders, and staff would report that you are credible, trustworthy, likeable, and capable of keeping confidences.

T or **F** If asked, you could easily identify three of your strengths or three of your weaknesses, and you consistently work toward improving those weaknesses.

T or **F** Because of your track record, others view you as a credible and trusted resource.

T or **F** You regularly read and understand your company's financials and their impact on business.

T or **F** You regularly read non-HR news publications and resources.

T or **F** You have partnered with and understand the needs of other departments in the organization.

T or **F** Peers and leaders seek to involve you in organizational taskforces and committees, not because they have to but because they want to.

T or **F** You have surfaced and implemented at least one new idea in the past 18 months.

T or **F** You have either implemented, are working under, or are working on a workforce plan for talent acquisition and employee engagement in your organization.

T or **F** You have built a network of and regularly engage with other HR professionals.

T or **F** You read at least two career-related books a year.

T or **F** You are (or are working toward) becoming a

certified professional, which requires you to stay current with changes in the profession.

T or **F** Regardless of whether you work in a global organization or have global HR responsibilities, you stay abreast of the potential impact of globalization on your company or industry.

T or **F** You are keenly aware of the needs of both your internal and your external customers and work to meet the needs of both.

Answering "false" to most of these statements means you are leading your career in a manner consistent with someone who lacks vision, focus, and purpose. It means that you might not be taking responsibility for managing your career in a way that could prove to be productive and worthwhile to you and to your organization. Now is the time to take a look at where you are and allow it to motivate you to soar to new heights and not be weighed down by indictment of past decisions. Your career in HR should do more than meet your immediate financial needs.

> *Every second a seeker can start over, for his life's mistakes are initial drafts and not the final version.*
>
> —Sri Chinmoy

Becoming an effective HR professional can offer financial security for you now and into the future, but you should be managing your career in HR to provide you with a sense of mental security as well, that should you lose this job, you are confident enough in your skills, abilities, attitude, and track record that you can find another rather easily. And finally, you should be managing your career so that your growth and development are apparent to you and to those you serve.

People with a vision have a roadmap for their success. They are confident, secure, and content regardless of the state they are in. They are future oriented while accounting for and meeting their immediate needs. Major winds of change or storms don't easily shake them because they have planned for and are prepared mentally, physically, and financially for any challenges that may come their way. This book is designed to help you get focused and create that roadmap for your success in HR. Just as the world has gotten more interactive, this book is hands-on, with questions, charts, worksheets, and more to help you take actual steps toward your HR goals, because in the end, taking action is what it's all about. The future of HR is brightest for HR professionals who are relevant, credible, trustworthy self-developers, who consistently bring their A game to the table. Work hard. Play hard.

CHAPTER ONE

HR Today

Successful and unsuccessful people do not vary greatly in their abilities. They vary in their desires to reach their potential.

—John Maxwell

What Is HR?

Human Resources used to be about processing paperwork and handling back office functions associated with moving people in or out of an organization. Not long ago, in fact, HR focused only on separating the wheat and tare in the organization, rewarding the high performers and culling the poor ones. Yes, HR used to be just about the people. Then something happened: we became increasingly important to the organization. So much so that the office changed names from Personnel to Human Resources, or the increasingly popular Chief People Office.

> *It is unfortunate when people allow themselves to get like concrete—all mixed up and permanently set.*
>
> —John Maxwell

Human Resources today involves the design of formal and informal processes, procedures, and systems used to acquire, engage, and inspire human capital in a way that leads to optimal organizational performance and achievement of goals. We are responsible for connecting the right people to systems and processes that get results.

What is different about today's HR professional is that to make the right connection, you have to be involved with and understand the operations of the business *and* be the, dare I say, "people person" of old. More than reviewing a job description, you have to understand the culture of the organization and the business units within it to help them obtain and maintain top talent. Today's HR professionals don't have to be finance, marketing, or information technology gurus, but they must be able to understand how all these operations (and others) work together to affect the bottom line and meet customer needs. In essence, they are the organization's glue when utilized effectively.

If you work in HR, let this be your lodestar for what you should be working toward in your HR organization. Getting there involves understanding the business, the economy, and how the two are interconnected. It also requires establishing benchmarks and metrics to lead your organization, and being a person of credibility and influence. How can you know where you want to go unless you establish a baseline for success, a that baseline starts with you?

Challenges Facing the Profession

Today's HR professional must successfully handle more challenges than ever before:
- Globalization
- Economic shifts
- Demographic changes to the workforce
- Information and social technology

- Legislative and governmental regulations
- Focus on the customer
- U.S. growth as a service provider and knowledge society
- Changing talent pool

All these influences and many more are impacting the world in which we live. The U.S. has gone from a highly industrial society to a leading world service provider. More specifically, these societal influences are influencing the where, the who, the how, and the what in the work we do. As recently as the late 90s, life was good. Employment was full, gas prices were climbing but manageable—after all, we'd always have work, right?

Then 9/11 occurred, we went to war, and the economy took a nose dive. We began recovering after banks and mortgage and other credit lenders began creatively identifying opportunities to obtain the American dream even for those who were previously not credit worthy. We were taking lavish trips, purchasing homes, and engaging in other nonessential activities that just made life good. Then a second wave hit in late 2008. That is when the recessionary tidal wave hit the U.S., and 3 years later we continue to struggle to dig our way out. In all of this, human resource professionals in the U.S. and in U.S.-based multinational corporations and enterprises were affected like never before. Mergers and acquisitions ensued. High-profile litigation of conglomerate business leaders consistently remained front page news, and their unethical behavior became the topic of many blog posts and newspaper and television headlines, not to mention the stuff keynote speeches are made of.

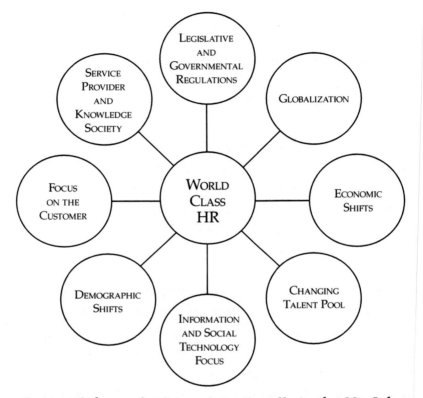

I entered the profession unintentionally in the 80s. It happened like this: I was working as an executive assistant and had five direct reports. It was part of my job to assist the executive director and, among other things, fill open positions, process paperwork, work with outside legal to address HR-related issues, and ensure that documents were filed properly. I recall many frustrating days and nights dealing with litigation (and litigation in healthcare is no picnic) and asking myself and legal counsel how we could avoid these situations in the future. He asked me if I seriously wanted to know, and thus began my journey into HR. He lit a match that has burned ever since. We discussed leadership, accountability, responsibility, rules, regulations, laws. I changed my major (as I was completing my undergraduate degree at the time) to business and human resources and have never looked back. He eventually became partner in a prestigious law firm based in Columbus, Ohio.

The profession is evolving, and many HR professionals will struggle to keep up if they don't begin to connect the dots shown on the page 12.

Demographic Shifts & the Changing Talent Pool

One of the most significant of all the dots above is likely to be demographic shifts. A recent report by the Bureau of Labor Statistics indicates that in 15–20 years, we could see as many as 14 million jobs sitting unfilled because of the lack of available qualified talent in the U.S.. In addition, according to a report by Deloitte, "In less than 20 years, roughly half of all workers in many of the world's most populous nations will come from Generation Y — the youngest generation of employees entering the workforce." Those graduates are entering the workforce with such tenacity and know-how that they are fiercely competitive and hungry for a chance to be effective and to change the world! They enter the workforce already having a sense of diversity, teamwork, and strong self-direction, not to mention their knowledge and application of

The secret of my success is a two word answer: Know people.

—Harvey S. Firestone

technology solutions. I call them the Point and Click generation—just point them in the direction they need to go and with one click of a keystroke, they will take off, many bringing back astounding results. HR's challenge? Keeping up with the Point and Click new entrants to the workforce and keeping them engaged. This generation doesn't want to sit in long classroom settings for training, nor are they interested in long stints of dues-paying career opportunities (who is these days anyway?). They don't know what it's like not having a microwave, computers, fast food restaurants, cell phones, or the Internet. So HR is challenged to keep up with and meet the P&C generation's expectations for a highly functioning organization and be prepared to receive all they have to offer.

Another point on the dot spectrum is the behavior of soon-to-retire Baby Boomers, those born between 1946 and 1964. They will not retire as rapidly as once thought but are seeking alternative career opportunities where they can work while partially retired or perhaps doing an entirely different type of job.

A huge dot on the continuum is that of the unemployed workforce: individuals who've felt the pain of the layoffs and downsizing over recent years and want to apply their skill set and strengths to either similar career paths or entirely different job functions. With the lens toward filling jobs expediently and efficiently, the challenge to HR is to take these mostly competent and skilled performers and figure out how their skills transfer to another type of job and making the love connection where career changers meet traditional hiring managers. Let's not forget to also mention that women and people of color are leaving the workforce to start businesses and aren't considering, at least at this juncture, being gainfully employed by anyone other than themselves.

Finally, there are the recession survivors: those indirectly affected by layoffs of co-workers, friends, and family, who feel guilty for surviving and continuing to be the income earners in their families. These people might feel fortunate to have their jobs, but don't you dare rub that in their faces. Innovative HR professionals are recognizing that these individuals also need attention and support and are finding ways to connect the frayed edges of these groups back into their organizations. This can be accomplished through work with EAP and employee engagement programs.

Legislative and Governmental Regulations

The continuing regulatory changes impacting the profession could very well affect how potential new entrants determine if they even want to work in HR as well as how companies value HR. Staying on top of ever-changing employment regulations and ensuring that they are effectively and appropriately applied and communicated in organizations is critical for HR success. In fact, the laws have so affected the workforce that according to the March 2011 *Harvard Business Review*, many CEOs are looking to licensed attorneys (among other traditionally non-HR functional leaders) to fulfill senior and executive level chief HR officer roles, formally awarded to long-time HR career professionals. There is a legal aspect to HR, yes, but tying legality to practical application is best left in the hands of credible HR practitioners, who can effectively prevent your Human Resources Department from turning into a courtroom.

Globalization

In the wake of global competition and the competitive landscape, the opportunities for HR professionals to partner with the organization as it expands its business globally will be vitally important. Being resourceful, capable, and willing to quickly adapt and adjust to the consistently changing world, and apply new learning to move business forward, is what the 21st century HR professional must do. Even though the U.S. faces talent shortages in the coming decade, the need for talent is not limited to the U.S.. Colleges and universities across the globe are feeding on the enthusiasm and talent of scholarly students in their junior and senior college years and luring them away to finish their education abroad in an effort to ensure the pipeline of talent is sufficient to sustain global economies. Young professionals who are seeking to fast-track their careers and have the flexibility and willingness to live abroad are finding global opportunities the best approach to broadening their professional scope.

Mandarin continues to be one of the fastest growing foreign languages being taught in secondary school, while China, Brazil, Africa, and India continue to snag our attention with the availability of human capital we so desperately need for entry level and executive level jobs. HR must be in a position to address the talent acquisition and retention needs of a global workforce and be in position to help their growing organization globalize its operations.

Economic Shifts

Emerging markets, consumer behavior, wars, and a focus on energy are all affecting and shifting the global economy. How HR responds to the new economy can very well dictate and become a predictor of organizational success. The workforce and unemployment market are made up of individuals who've been affected in some way economically. Who doesn't know someone who has been negatively impacted by changes in the economy? Who isn't familiar with the conflicts taking place across the world? Who hasn't read an article or viewed a broadcast on the growth in India or opportunities that expand in Brazil and Africa?

In addition, oil prices continue to affect how we think about going from point A to point B. In all of this, the job of today's human resource professional must be to mitigate any negative impact on the organization. People don't leave their personal life at the door anymore (I doubt they ever did), and so the attitudes of workers current and future are being shaped by the economic impact on them personally. Negative impacts create fear and distrust in the minds of those most affected. So while we are focused on assessing the organizational effects of these economic shifts (and we very well should be), we must also keep in mind and address the cultural influence on the workforce. Establishing work/ life fit programs that address the needs of former dual-income families will be an accommodation that will extend the longevity of your best performers. In addition, continuing to offer financial management and education programs for employees and their families will not only help them

9

recover from the impact of the recession but will endear them to their caring employer.

Information and Social Technology

The implications for HR professionals in this arena are clear: get on board and keep up with the pace. Technology could very well be a game changer for many businesses willing to grow and find success and sustainability into the future. According to InternetWorldStats.com, 44% of worldwide Internet users are found in Asia, 22% in Europe, and North America follows at 12%. So if a business wanted to reach a global market quickly, wouldn't it stand to reason that they might look to the Internet as a means of doing so?

The key for human resource professionals will be to understand the business needs and implications, and perhaps help the company identify ways technology could boost profit or create an entirely new approach to doing business. Sometimes it is as simple as asking, "How can this be done better?" to get to the next best thing. HR can create opportunities for this to occur and to tap into the intellect of technologically savvy employees who can then become the think tank for new business ideas. The future of business needs HR professionals who are not afraid of technology, who are willing to embrace its capabilities and utilize available human capital to tap into and explore its potential for business success.

Service Provider and Knowledge Society

Services produced by private industry account for almost

70% of the U.S. GDP. The fastest growing service sectors are durable goods manufacturing—computers and electronics, real estate, financial services; professional, scientific, and technical services; and health care. Let's add to that the argument by Peter Drucker that there is a transition from a society based on material goods to one based on information or knowledge. The impact of these changes likely stems from the increase in service providers and the ease with which they can be marketed and consumed through electronic media.

These changes have made it easier for burgeoning entrepreneurs to go into business and become formidable competitors with large and even international organizations. Perhaps this is the reason we are seeing more women and minority entrepreneurs. In fact, according to the U.S. Census Bureau, the minority business community has grown at a faster rate than the minority population, and faster than all other US firms. Minority-owned firms nearly doubled from 3 million in 1997 to 5.8 million in 2007. The Census Bureau reports, "Success in the minority business community leads to job creation, an expanded tax base, community benefits and global competitiveness."

When you consider the implications of the retiring Baby Boom population over the years, and the continued growth rate of women- and minority-owned businesses, you can see that organizations will look to HR to help solve their talent crisis. Where will the talent come from? An obvious opportunity will be to engage and embrace those with an entrepreneurial spirit while they are still employed, giving them the freedom to expand, grow, and develop on company time and using company resources, as well as rewarding and compensating them equitably and fairly in the process.

Focus on the Customer

With the obvious increase and rise in the service sector, the focus on customer engagement and service is critical to company success and growth. The rise in for-profit membership and loyalty-type programs, customer appreciation rewards and discount programs, and "have it your way" customer service means that not only are the customers always right, but they have the branded tattoo to prove it.

There are simply too many choices for a customer to not find satisfaction and service on their first stop. Adopt the car salesperson's attitude that if they walk off the lot and don't buy a car, you've lost them to a competitor. They won't be back. We have one shot to get it right with our customers. In HR, you have to be in the forefront to ensure that staff members are attracting the customers and keeping them happy, satisfied, and spending their disposable income with your company. Selection is just part of HR's responsibility. Today, it's not just the front desk clerk who needs customer service training—*everyone* needs to know who the customers are, what they like and dislike, how they want to be served, and when. If you aren't a 24/7 company, you better behave like one in order to keep up. HR's role is to ensure that everyone is drinking the customer service Kool-aid.

Connecting all of these dots is the focus and the future facing HR.

How are you addressing these impacts in your organization? How have you grown professionally as a result?

Have you implemented anything new or enhanced any programs or services in the last 2-3 years to address these business trends?

Career Challenges of the HR Professional

If you work in HR long enough you are likely to experience or have experienced one or more of these concerns commonly shared by many professionals:

- Lack of career mobility
- Lack of mobility in company
- Frustration with always being the "bad guy"
- Not reporting to the CEO
- Feeling pigeonholed in the HR role
- Lack of support for HR initiatives at the top
- Lack of career development opportunities
- Not enough time in the day
- Feeling that HR is not a respected role in your company
- No peer support or professional network
- Being judged against popular HR success stories: Southwest, Zappos, SAS, Google, etc.

Even the best HR professionals have experienced these career challenges. Perhaps what makes some HR professionals better than others is the ability to see beyond current circumstances, to focus on their own career development, to change what they can, and to manage around the rest. Not everyone can "do" HR, and it is never the same function in any two organizations. Expect some different brand of HR everywhere you go. If you are a complainer who lacks the ability to take charge of your career and need to be hoisted up on someone's shoulder every time you have incremental success, HR is *not* for you. Turn and run as fast as you can.

A successful man is one who can lay a firm foundation with the bricks others have thrown at him.

—David Brinkley

Tough-minded, self-guided learners who are not afraid to stand alone are what great HR is made of. We work long or odd hours. We pat *ourselves* on the back, or get our network to do it for us, and we find the time for career development for free or for fee. Today's successful HR professional is influential and credible. The best HR professionals know how to leverage their company brand, elevate the HR role in the company, and leave a legacy behind. When they leave the company, they are missed, and the feeling is that no one can fill their shoes. When they join a new company, their positive reputation precedes them, and they are highly sought after regardless of their level in an organization. *This* is great HR, and this is what this book is about. It is for those willing to put the time into managing their career to a level of excellence that most will never attain. You can get there if you are willing to put the time in.

Chapter Review

What other career challenges are you facing?

Can you think of someone who meets the description in the paragraph above? Is he or she part of your network? Describe who this person is and what you most admire. Send him or her a note.

CHAPTER TWO

Why Choose a Career in HR?

Destiny is not a matter of chance; it is a matter of choice. It is not a thing to be waited for; it is a thing to be achieved.

—William Jennings Bryan

Why HR?

Let me start out by saying that HR as a profession is not for everyone. There are at least three groups of HR professionals in my experience:

Group 1:   Born and Raised
These individuals went to college and for some reason, either by intent or by accident, decided on a degree in HR and upon graduation were fortunate to get a job in HR and have decided never to leave. Also in this category are individuals we'll call career HR professionals, who might have stumbled into HR after college but loved it so much that their career aspiration is to be the top HR professional in their organization of choice. There are legacy professionals with no formal HR education that

worked in HR back when it was Personnel but grew and developed along the way. These HR professionals will retire as, hopefully, celebrated HR professionals (though this is not always the case).

Group 2:   Passing Through
These individuals stumbled upon HR, liked it as a career choice after college or after working in other parts of business, and thought they'd park for a while. Ultimately, these individuals have set their sights on working in another part of the business and see HR as a step toward that goal. Many make terrific HR professionals for the long run, and because of their lengthy stint in HR, they might not be viewed as passing through; however, if you follow their track record, even 10–15 years for them is just passing through. These are the type of individuals who, if they practiced HR successfully, are best to move into COO, CEO, or other senior level roles.

Group 3:   Sentenced
These individuals were forced into HR because of lack of success in other parts of the organization, or because someone actually thought they would be good working with "people" (as if to say they couldn't do so with machines, heavy equipment, or the public in general). Some will find success in HR after the sentencing, but others, well, they will not. For those unfortunate people working in a company with "sentenced" HR professionals... I'm sorry.

Of course there are various shades of gray to these categories, and it is not only possible but realistic to find success and failure with each of the categories above. These categories speak more to the attitude of the professional and less to the actual skill of the person. If someone is committed to work in HR, he or she can find success with the right attitude and a good fit with the company.

Your job is to ensure that you have the mindset for HR and the attitude it takes to run an effective HR program. The challenge for many a company is in making sure they hire the right fit to lead their HR team. Certification and practical hands-on experience with a list of accomplishments is a great start, but hiring managers and CEOs must diligently look at candidates' track record and probe their career aspirations to determine which HR professional is best for their organization. Today's HR professionals must have passion for what they are doing, which shows up in their attitude, reputation, and results. They have to want to be in HR. It's a tough job, and you want someone who can handle the job and is resolute in this role for the company.

The least attractive of the three is the "sentenced" group. People who are working out a sentence do not keep up with the changes in regulations and rely heavily on others in the organization to help discharge their HR responsibilities— legal counsel, finance, marketing, etc. They are basically biding their time until released, and it shows in their attitude and in the HR program itself. An HR program run by a number of "sentenced" HR people (can't quite call them professionals) remains in the status quo, operates in a passive mode, and is more reactionary in approach to HR challenges. These HR

> *Expect problems and eat them for breakfast.*
> —Alfred A. Montapert

employees don't quite make the connection between external influences and business realities.

If you find that you are not progressive and forward thinking, keeping up with the profession and driving appropriate change, or making realistic and appropriate business decisions, then you need to stop and reevaluate if HR is the right career for you. HR by definition really is a forward-thinking and progressive profession, not static by any stretch of the imagination.

Working with People

One way or another, you've heard the phrase "I just like working with people." Either that came out of your mouth (if you're willing to admit it) or you heard it come from another person seeking an opportunity to work with you in human resources.

Truth is, there are lots of areas in human resources where you rarely have to work with a single person. If you are technologically savvy and enjoy computers more than people, you can work in the Human Resource Information Systems area of an organization. There are transactional jobs in human resources that require you to process data and manage systems, and you still would be considered as part of the Human Resources Department. Then there are the more traditional responsibilities that involve lots of interaction with people, including everything from recruiting and new hire orientation to training and employee relations. HR has changed over the years, and thanks to globalization and technology, it is reinventing itself almost daily. So, why HR *today*?

At the core working in human resources as a deliberate career choice is the satisfaction you get from having a positive impact on the lives of those who work in your organization. You enjoy seeing things change and improve and the idea of helping to build a family of individuals who work together to make things happen in a big way. If you make a good hire, you take credit for "finding" that person for the organization. If you make a bad hire, the person is often referred back to human resources to "fix" and bandage up—in this case, you are the nurse and the Human Resources Department is the hospital.

It takes all kinds of people to work in an organization and to work together to achieve goals. HR can really be like a box of chocolates, where you sometimes never know what you're gonna get. Maybe that's the appeal, the element of surprise at seeing someone grow and flourish and receiving credit for it.

People come to work in an organization with all kinds of baggage. Using psychological analysis to weed out the bad seeds isn't foolproof. Trust me on this one. To work in HR today takes courage and tenacity. Some days the people will love you and hoist you up on their shoulders, and other days they'll drag your good name through the mud. If you can deal with the ups and downs of people and their emotions, you will love working in human resources. If you don't have tough skin and can't handle it when you're not the most popular kid on the block that week, get out and run to another career field. HR is not for the weak minded. You have to be tough and willing to take a tough stance and some hard knocks from time to time. You must also be a continuous learner, because the rules and regulations affecting our field keep changing and you *must* keep up if you want to keep your job.

The good news, there is plenty of variety in human resources. Don't abandon HR simply because you had one bad experience. Could it be you just didn't have the right HR job fit for your skill set and interest? Not everyone can generalize, and not everyone can specialize. There is a lot of varied work to do in HR, and before you dare think of giving up or getting out, try on another HR discipline for size.

Explore the Different Areas of HR Focus

According to the Society for Human Resource Management (SHRM), there are at least 13 different disciplines in the human resource field:

- Benefits Administration
- Business Leadership
- Compensation
- Consulting
- Diversity
- Employee Relations
- Ethics and Sustainability
- Global HR
- Labor Relations
- Organizational and Employee Development
- Safety and Security
- Talent Acquisition and Staffing Management
- Technology

Embedded in this list are probably employment law and employee health and welfare, but let's call them out and describe them separately:

Benefits Administration
Managing indirect rewards given to employees of an organization.

Business Leadership
Coordinating activities that lead to the engagement and development of human capital to achieve short- and long-term organizational goals.

Compensation
Managing systems in organizations that reward people for work through pay and benefits.

Consulting
Providing professional advice, guidance, and information to organizations on a contractual basis.

Diversity
Acknowledging differences among people who work together and leveraging those differences to achieve organizational goals.

Employee Relations
Ensuring that the organization creates a work environment fostering productivity and positive employee interaction.

Employee Health and Welfare
Ensuring employees are physically and emotionally fit to perform in work activities and that the work environment is free from health-related hazards.

Ethics and Sustainability
Conveying organizational and personal values and their expression in business decision making and behavior.

This discipline emphasizes organizational codes of ethics but includes relevant legal requirements. It also deals with the social impact of business decisions. (See SHRM Online)

Global HR

Dealing with all aspects of HR within the worldwide context, including U.S.-based entities doing business internationally and non-U.S.-based entities operating in their own locale or worldwide. (See SHRM Online)

Labor Relations

Overseeing elements of formal labor-management relations—protected activities, unfair practices, union organizing, recognition and representation elections—as well as collective bargaining and contract administration. (See SHRM Online)

Organizational and Employee Development

Dealing with the performance of the organization and how human capital is developed to make a positive contribution to organizational outcomes.

Safety and Security

Ensuring the physical protection of employees while engaging in work-related activity and in employer owned and operated facilities. Also involves the protection and maintenance of employer property and equipment.

Talent Acquisition and Staffing Management

Working with strategies around acquisition, retention, and engagement of human capital for an organization.

Technology

Dealing with systems required to manage human

capital information and to facilitate technology-driven employment-related transactions.

Employment Law

Ensuring that rules, regulations, business practices, organizational culture, and company policy are compliant with local, federal, and international law as applicable. Also involves ensuring the proper interpretation, application, and communication of employment laws internally.

These 15 areas of HR can then be divided into 3 main categories:

Rules and Regulations

These HR disciplines are directly and significantly affected by employment laws and regulations. Individuals working in these jobs must have a propensity toward law because regulatory changes occur routinely and attention to detail is required.

- Employment Law
- Benefits Administration
- Compensation
- Labor Relations
- Safety and Security

Employee Engagement

Individuals working in these disciplines relish interaction with others and are capable of building and sustaining relationships with people.

- Consulting
- Diversity
- Employee Relations

- Employee Health and Welfare
- Organizational and Employee Development
- Staffing Management

Leadership

These areas of human resources involve strategic agility, foresight, innovation, and the ability to help organizations be trend savvy. Individuals working in these areas must have a track record or demonstrated ability to work through people to accomplish goals as well as a reputation for being a fair and unbiased leader.

- Business Leadership
- Ethics and Sustainability
- Global HR
- Technology

What Makes a Good HR Professional?

There's lots of discussion these days about who makes the best HR professional. Is it someone who went to undergraduate school and graduated with a degree in HR and then moved into HR and stayed committed throughout his or her career? Or is it someone who completed a nontraditional degree program, perhaps working in other jobs before landing in HR? Hiring individuals into HR that have not been through the school of HR will likely always be hotly contested. The answer: it depends.

Consider this: hiring someone who was trained *professionally* and even has work experience as a statistician will likely harvest an employee working in HR that has a bent toward metrics and measures. Hiring someone who was trained and obtained work in a marketing role could result in an employee working in HR that has a bent toward the buying and selling aspects of running the business. All of these attributes are good for HR and can successfully make a positive contribution to the work in the organization, but anyone working in HR should be well versed and trained in the profession. If you are looking at such employees in or for your HR department, then I offer these ideas for consideration:

Take these individuals through a rigorous process of formal HR training.

- Create a performance management plan to ensure there is alignment and consistent balance between their prior experience and the expectations of the job.
- Consider HR certification training and HR certification.
- Give them the opportunity to apply their prior experience to their current job in HR. You can benefit from the experience of these nontraditional new entrants, but you must ensure there is balance to prevent overuse in a particular area.
- If you are planning to fill an HR opening from a pool of nontraditional candidates, look for individuals who could add value to your existing program. Hiring a person with prior marketing, finance, project management, and technology experience could be the key to taking your HR organization to an even higher level.

If you believe you have skills that are transferrable to HR, then consider taking these steps:

- Enroll in an HR course at the local college or university.
- Talk to individuals already working successfully in the profession.
- Conduct an informational interview and discuss how your skills could be transferred into HR and how to address any roadblocks you might encounter.
- Be willing to start at the entry level in the hiring organization's HR Department.
- Make sure your cover letter makes it clear how your skill set is transferrable to HR.
- If offered an interview, don't leave without addressing how your skills are transferrable and how you can add value to the existing department.
- Don't accept a job in HR that requires you to be brainwashed into HR and forget or dismiss your past experience. The value you bring is your complementary skill set. You must ensure you are able to connect your prior experiences to your HR job, which will require practice and application. It won't be perfect, but a process of trial and error demands the opportunity to at least give it a try. But remember that your new love is HR—your prior non-HR experience is now your mistress.

HR Area of
Concentration Assessment

Now, let's examine which of these areas might be best suited for you. Check only one letter from each group that best describes you—choose only A, B, or C.

	A	Can be inspirational and motivational for individuals, work groups, business units or even the organization.
	B	Likes to work with others to identify and resolve challenges. Is adept at seeking hidden resolutions.
	C	Prefers to design processes, procedures and the rules that govern interaction. Is technically adept and looks for ways to use technology to enhance work.

	A	Has a futuristic conversation and can talk beyond current circumstances or situations and creates inspired vision and a sense of purpose.
	B	Is skilled at paying attention while in conversation so as to pick up on the main points and restate them accurately.
	C	Is known for strengths with written communication. Conveys written messages that are concise when needed and that accomplish the intended purpose.

	A	Determined and dedicated to ensure internal and external customers receive high-quality programs, products, and service.
	B	Is known for relating well to people regardless of position, level in or outside of organization, or relationship status. Is tactful, patient and capable of diffusing negative situations or circumstances with ease.
	C	Is a good team member known for seeking and providing the information people need to effectively discharge their job responsibilities.

	A	Is comfortable empowering others to accomplish goals and creates an environment open to creativity and innovation.
	B	Is known as trustworthy and demonstrates morale character and honesty. Is truthful, shares opinions without intentionally offending others and has a reputation for keeping confidences.
	C	Is patient and offers quiet and steady perseverance when dealing with processes and with people. Seeks to understand before being understood and ensures established processes and procedures are followed before taking action.

	A	Can anticipate and forecast local and global trends with accuracy and use detail to create strategies and plans. Keenly aware of the competition and competitive analysis.
	B	Is skilled at identifying and tapping the right people for the right task or assignments. Ensures a diverse talent mix is considered in selection processes and considers the needs of internal and external clients in placement recommendations.
	C	Has solid reputation for being a good decision-maker. Is one people tend to seek for advice and counsel. Draws upon personal and professional experience, analysis of data, and sound judgment to ensure good decision quality.

	A	Can maintain composure in difficult and confrontational situations. Isn't easily offended, manages stress and crisis situations well. Is a calming force during tough times.
	B	Has a reputation and track record for establishing and maintaining strong internal and external customer relationships. Has excellent customer orientation, and can discern the need to communicate changes or improvements to enhance the customer experience.
	C	Track record for successfully maneuvering through difficult situations or negotiations to bring about satisfying resolutions to all parties. Finds satisfaction with their ability to help others settle their differences with minimal negative impact on existing relationships.

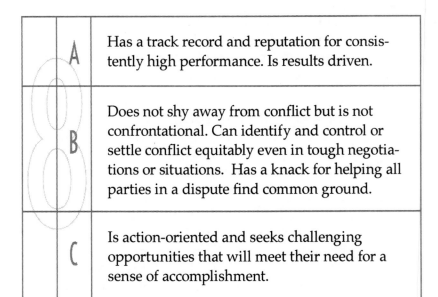

A		Has a track record and reputation for consistently high performance. Is results driven.
	B	Does not shy away from conflict but is not confrontational. Can identify and control or settle conflict equitably even in tough negotiations or situations. Has a knack for helping all parties in a dispute find common ground.
	C	Is action-oriented and seeks challenging opportunities that will meet their need for a sense of accomplishment.

A		Has a track record and reputation for consistently high performance. Is results driven.
	B	Does not shy away from conflict but is not confrontational. Can identify and control or settle conflict equitably even in tough negotiations or situations. Has a knack for helping all parties in a dispute find common ground.
	C	Is action-oriented and seeks challenging opportunities that will meet their need for a sense of accomplishment.

	A	Holds to personal and corporate values. Rewards, recognizes and acknowledges the behaviors and practices that are in line with corporate culture.
	B	People find this person easy to approach. Often referred to as friendly, easy to meet, good listener, receptive, warm and settling.
	C	Is skilled at accomplishing work and achieving goals through both formal and informal networks within an organization or business unit.

	A	Knows how to create a performance driven environment and can adjust style to meet needs of individual contributors.
	B	Has a reputation for being able to relate to people regardless of their race, age, ability, culture, creed, professional background, family history, etc. Also known for making inclusive business and hiring decisions. Is comfortable and effective in positive and negatively charged diversity related situations.
	C	Does well when faced with challenges and can quickly adapt to change when needed. Enjoys changes in daily routine especially when it involves finding solutions or process improvement.

	A	Has leadership courage and is willing to take on responsibilities others might avoid and perform well. Is not afraid to take adverse action even if s/he has to stand alone.
	B	Can quickly identify and maneuver through the politics (both internal and external) that are part of an organizations culture or that impact the work in an organization. Is adept at helping others understand and adjust to the maze of politics for a more productive work experience.
	C	Is comfortable around individuals in more senior positions in an organization. Conveys messages and communicates with them at their level when needed and is capable of communicating with people regardless of level in the organization. A strength would be in the ability to understand and convey complex rules to different audiences.

Count the total number of A's, B's, and C's from above:

A's = _____

B's = _____

C's = _____

Results

A's = Leadership

If most of your results contained A's, then you are likely already in a leadership position and looking for greater challenge or ready to move into a leadership position. The key here will be to ensure that you enjoy working at a high level in an organization and are a good leader of leaders. If you currently work in a leadership position, this will be less of a difficult transition than if you currently do not have supervisory accountability or responsibility for individuals or major strategic initiatives.

Making the transition from middle manager to director level or higher can be tough. Depending on the type of organization and the organizational culture, the actual HR job responsibility can be vastly different. In smaller organizations HR directors and higher often must have more tactical responsibilities than they would like simply because the resources are scarce; whereas in larger organizations, where resources are less scarce, individuals at the director level and above can take more of a strategic approach to leadership, which means you must be able to stay out of the weeds!

If you are a leader, please let your leaders lead and your staff do their jobs. Advise and inquire if you must, but don't jump into the day-to-day. Consistently breathing down the neck of capable HR professionals will be a distraction, and it will signal that you don't trust them to do the work and deliver on results. If members of your team are not delivering on results, then deal with the behavior, but you can do that and still not get in the weeds. If you must *know* what they are doing, ask for them to conduct a time study and work analysis over a short work cycle (usually less than 30 days). But do this only if you *must,* as it is time consuming and distracting for the worker. Oh, yeah—you could also just ask.

Contrary to popular belief, great leaders don't necessarily have to do or have done the work of those for which they have accountability and responsibility. They must, however, be capable of marshaling human capital, technology, and other resources to accomplish organizational goals without having to do the work themselves. The best leaders know what they don't know and find a way to fill the gap. In addition, ensuring that you function and build credibility as an ethical leader who seeks the good of the whole rather than just building your own reputation or skill set will secure a team of supportive staff.

Leadership is more than a position: it involves understanding the connection between a complex set of variables that may or may not seem related and making them work together for positive results. Current and future human resource leaders must be willing to continue to take a stand for what is right, in the face of opposition, even if they stand alone. You can disagree respectfully, and sometimes you'll have to pull staff and peers along kicking and screaming, but that is the core of what makes great leaders. That is what they do.

> *Good leaders take people where they want to go, but great leaders take people, not necessarily where they want to go but where they need to be.*
>
> —Rosalind Carter

Ensuring the sustainability of your organization's future is not just the CEO's job. HR has to be on the lookout for future opportunities and the negative implications of business decisions or the absence of sound judgment. As one CEO told me in a former HR role, "Pam, you're the conscience of this organization. You keep us honest and focused." Ensuring sustainability may mean introducing your company to something new. Leaders get ahead of change; they don't just follow it.

Consider your answers to these questions:

- What are you reading to enhance, sustain, and influence your HR leadership thinking?
- Who are you adding to your network to help you grow and develop?
- How are you expanding and exposing your HR global consciousness?
- Who is holding you ethically and morally accountable both personally and professionally?
- How are you developing your leadership capabilities?

B's = Employee Engagement

Now if you had more B's in your total, you tend to prefer work that involves employee and customer engagement. Employee relations, training, employee development, diversity and inclusion, and talent acquisition are the types of HR job families you might find interesting. Another option for you would be to consider consulting or a job that involves a lot of external customer contact.

You might enjoy responsibilities such as:

- sourcing candidates and conducting interviews
- training people managers
- delivering presentations or training to both internal and external audiences in a formal or classroom environment

- coordinating the on-boarding process
- developing strategies and systems that govern employee and customer-related work
- managing the culture by addressing employee issues and concerns
- establishing and leading mentoring and succession planning programs
- governing internal committees

This list isn't exhaustive but a sample of the types of things individuals that enjoy employee and customer interaction can expect to encounter in a job situation. The key to this area is ensuring that you operate with diplomacy, tact, trust, and confidentiality when applicable. The HR department and function must be seen as a resource to internal customers and external customers—a place that epitomizes the nature of work-life in the organization. At the heart of HR are those individuals who manage the employee interaction throughout the organization. We must act as both the sounding board and the bull horn when needed and when not wanted. HR is in essence the heartbeat of the organization. We control and hold the culture in our hands, and having worked in organizations with bad HR practices and poor HR leadership, I can tell you that not having a handle on the culture and how it can affect the top and bottom lines can be the coup de grace to an otherwise great organization.

C's = Rules and Regulations

More total C's in your response means you are the human resource rule maker and rule follower. I am a card-carrying member of this club and occasionally flash my card proudly. Writing policies and debating union stewards are things you do or would like to do with ease and precision.

More C's doesn't mean you should pursue a law degree; it just means you are adept at establishing and getting others to follow policies, practices, and procedures. The HR department of today must ensure it stays abreast of the changes in local and national law. HR professionals today must understand and be able to interpret, articulate, and effectively communicate the implications of governance and employment law to a wide variety of audiences. This also means that individuals working in this rules-and-regulations-governed area must be technologically agile, have strong oral and written communication skills, and be quick learners and change agents. You have to be able to build relationships and bridges in this area of HR simply because, though you may or may not make the rules, you communicate the rules, and often it's the mailman that gets bit by the dog.

Why is this area such a tough area of work? Benefits, compensation, labor relations, and health, safety, and security all touch people personally. These areas affect how they live their lives. If a step is overlooked or a policy not properly communicated, or a change not implemented properly, you could jeopardize someone's health, income, or even their life. It is important to not just have an aptitude for this area; you have to have a personality and attitude for it. You must be on top of your game as it relates to your customer service attitude. Returning calls, making yourself available to explain policy to family members, being available outside normal work hours are all part of working in this area. If you don't possess a great deal of patience, empathy, and self-control, regardless of your level in these areas, this is probably not an area you should consider.

Also, this area isn't just about keeping the law. It is also about seeking to establish policies, benefits, practices, and procedures that promote a better work environment. If FMLA says 12 weeks of time off, why not offer 14 weeks? Go above and beyond for your employees and they will go above and beyond for you. I'll never forget going to an interview and discussing how much money I had saved an employer in benefits costs. I was so proud of those accomplishments until the interviewer said to me, "Pam, that is nice that you saved the company money, but what did you do to promote a better work environment through benefits and compensation? We have money to spend to enhance our benefit and compensation program, and we're looking for someone who has a track record for enhancing our total compensation package, not cutting it!" Wow, talk about a reality check. After looking at him as if he spoke in Ter Sami (a language spoken in Russia by fewer than 2 people), I realized that I had this whole thing wrong. Clearly, I didn't get that job, but I learned a valuable lesson that would reshape how I viewed my role as an HR professional.

HR is about helping people who serve others. The best that I could do as a professional was, yes, stay on top of the rules and regulations, but more important, make my organization one that people would not want to leave, and if they did, they'd want to come back. Not just because of the benefits and the compensation but because I had helped to create a culture where people *wanted* to be. That was my job then, and that is my job today. If we do our job right, leaders will look for people who are business savvy, not just HR savvy, to take the top HR seats in their organizations—attorneys and marketing professionals have the right to take the top HR seat, but only if we give it to them.

Equal A's, B's, and C's = Generalist

If you had a pretty equal number in all three categories, then you are likely currently performing as a generalist or a new entrant to the HR workforce. You probably have a bent toward doing a little bit of everything that HR has to offer. Someone might argue that "generalist" is not a category. After all, a generalist is a person not at all focused in one or a few primary areas of HR but must know something about all aspects of HR. This is absolutely true. As a generalist HR professional myself, I needed to know something about and execute strategy in all aspects of HR. However, even as a generalist, there is a primary area of interest that drives each HR professional. We all have our HR bent. Your HR bent is typically your proclivity or partiality toward a specific thing or area of focus. I might like home improvement but am more partial to painting. I might enjoy yard work but prefer to focus most on plants and flowers than mowing and edging.

If you watch carefully, you can determine even a generalist's bent; it tends to be the area of HR he or she focuses most on. To an extreme, it can show up as being uncaring for things outside that particular area. For example, if I like yard work but focus primarily on the plants and flowers, what happens to my grass and the trees? They suffer from neglect (not to mention the complaints from neighbors). In the world of HR a professional HR generalist who has an overused bias toward employment law, for example, might keep his or her

41

organization out of the court system but could perhaps be applying a legal lens toward something that is more relational
in nature, thereby turning HR into a courtroom, and who
wants to visit a court of law every time they have a need?

Chapter Review

What do you think about your results?

*Are your results in line with your general feel for how you
could focus your HR career?*

*How do your results compare with others assessments you've
taken?*

CHAPTER THREE

Setting Your Compass

Do not go where the path may lead, go instead
where there is no path and leave a trail.

—Ralph Waldo Emerson

Where Are You Going?

The fight between knowing where you think you want to go and deciding which path or paths to take is a battle you'll wage over and over. It's not that you can't decide between two simple roads; it's that life happens. Circumstances change, people change, we live, we grow, we change our minds, we fall in and out of love, we have kids, we deal with death, we get our hearts broken, we work for great people, then bad people, our financial situation fluctuates, and did I mention life happens? These circumstances and many more influence how we think about our future. The best thing you can do is to first decide, "Where do I want to be at the end of this road?" Now that can change too, but at least you'll have set your compass!

Your compass is your mindset. It is the thing that helps you stay focused. This means that in the midst of "life happening," you know that your compass continues to be set on your ultimate goal. Let me give you an example. When

I decided to embark on an HR career, I was working in a company as the Jack of all trades. I was an executive assistant with 5 direct reports, managing 3 boards: a governing board and two community services boards—for the same company. I ran the fundraising program (including concerts, golf outings, and all the fundraising campaigns) *and* was the resident HR guru. Clearly, I couldn't say "no." I have to say I *loved it*, but I was quickly getting burned out. I needed out and had to decide on a career path: HR, because of all the different hats I was wearing, HR was the one that spoke to me, the one where I found the greatest professional satisfaction, and the one where I saw a career with longevity.

So I finished my undergraduate degree and sought a job that was *just* HR. For that period, my compass was set on finishing my degree and obtaining a *real HR job*. I would continue to deal with life by burning the wick at both ends, amid the flurry that comes from wearing multiple hats, moving full steam ahead to finish my degree, because my focus was on getting a real HR job. Did I mention that I got married just a few classes shy of finishing my degree? Getting married and dealing with all these things were not interruptions or distractions because not only did I know that my compass was set on finishing my degree and getting a real HR job, but I made it known to those who needed to be in the know (my boss, my fiancé, my family, and my closest friends), so they would help me stay on course.

Staying focused was a battle that was very real for me. There were those that told me I was trying to do too much. I needed to hold off on my degree or marriage or both. I was told to stay with that employer—it was a great job and could lead somewhere. There were supportive and unsupportive co-workers and staff. It was the unsupportive ones who really helped me know I was headed in the right direction, and thus the secret to winning the battle. Would there be a fight if you weren't headed in the right direction? I love, love, love this quote by Gandhi because it is so applicable for me at various stages in my life:

"First they ignore you, then they laugh at you, then they fight you, and then *you win!*" [emphasis mine]

When you are doing all the right things—building relationships, establishing credibility, improving yourself personally and professionally—and you constantly run into road blocks, especially those put up by other people, keep moving forward—that is the exact road you need to be on. I'm dyslexic when it comes to opposition. I always ask myself, "Why don't they think I should do this?" Or "Why aren't they giving me the opportunity to grow in this area?" or even, "Why won't they give me exposure to certain people, growth opportunities, experiences?" What about, "Why are they fighting me on this?" I find that when you have potential, other people see it and make it their personal mission to keep you from surpassing them. They don't always know it or recognize why they oppose or fight you; some just do it because they don't like you or because they really do think you are off base.

> *Leap, and the net will appear.*
>
> *—John Burroughs*

One of my favorite scenes is from the film *Love and Basketball*, in which a freshman female ball player on the team is highly competitive and has tremendous skills but a bad attitude. A senior teammate gives her hell and continues to bring out the freshman's bad attitude, keeps setting her up for failure until eventually the freshman gets her act together. When the senior injures herself in a game, the coach puts in the freshman, and she helps to win the game. The senior comes over to her on crutches in the locker room and says, "Never let a freshman take your spot." That was the senior's personal philosophy. She didn't like the fact that a freshman ball player had skills that would get her a starting spot—and she faced that fear year after year throughout college. Imagine the hell she gave other freshmen ball players because of her fear. Many times this type of fear becomes a self-fulfilled prophecy.

That is what many of you will face in your HR careers, and you'll see it played out over and over in your organizations with other people. When people have not set their compass on achieving their own professional or personal goals, when they do not have a sense of purpose and direction, they might feel stuck, directionless, or they might just want to stay where they are until retirement or until the next thing just happens to come along.

It's our nature: Human beings like success but they hate successful people.

—Carrot Top

It could also be that they do have a desire to achieve success and see you as a threat to getting there. What if you are both trying to achieve the same goal in the same company? In this case, there is bound to be conflict. Instead of turning your frustration or fear toward the other person, focus on your own self-development. It could be that your compass is pointed in the right direction but that your opportunities will not be internal but external. People are bound to get jealous or feel threatened by people with passion, purpose, and goals—it is a fact of life! When you have passion and purpose and are working toward *something*, you should expect opposition; just don't fail to rework your plan to go around it. The other thing to keep in mind is to not be overconfident, arrogant, or conceited in your attitude. There is nothing worse than getting off course or derailed and realizing you're to blame for the negative circumstances.

When setting your compass, think about more than just your career goal. Consider also your life goals or your mission or vision for your life. It should inspire you to act and stay focused. It must be bigger than you, and you have to put effort into getting there. As one person said, success means nothing if failure isn't an option. If you think you might be fortunate enough to move from work to retirement someday, shouldn't you start planning for it now? You're an HR professional—take your own advice for crying out loud! Read the headlines about where social security is headed and take an assessment of how much money you'll need to live on if you retire at your normal retirement age. For some of us, there is a huge gap, isn't there? Given this information alone, there are some questions you need to stop and answer before setting the dial on your compass:

End Game Summary

Given what I know today, my ideal retirement date is: ____/____/____

At the time of my retirement I will be age: _____

When I retire, I plan to work: _____ part-time until _____ or _____ as a volunteer _____ hours/day _____ days/week for this type of company _____

_____ not at all

My lifestyle activities while in retirement will include (biking, traveling, golf, reading, sewing, swimming, skiing, etc):

I plan to retire living in:

    _____ my current community, city, or someplace nearby

    _____ in an entirely different state or country

When I retire, my living arrangements will be:

    _____ retirement community

    _____ living with a relative

    _____ living in a single family home or apartment

Ideally, I'll still drive while in retirement:

    _____ Yes _____No _____ Maybe

My income will primarily come from (check all that apply):

    _____ PersonalSavings

    _____ Social Security

    _____ IRA

    _____ Pension

    _____ Investment Earnings

_____ Lottery and Bingo Earnings

_____ Other: _____

I have a personal financial advisor: _____ Yes _____ No

The box above is probably the most important section in this book. If you haven't thought about how you'll spend retirement, or even thought about retirement at all, then how do you know if your current career efforts are taking you in the right direction? Let the answers to the questions above guide you to your success. Don't wait until you're a few years from retirement to *start* thinking about and planning for it. That's like dreaming of taking a trip to Europe, believing the opportunity will present itself and never planning for it. Here's how to start:

1. Talk to someone you trust who is handling their finances reasonably well to help you collect names of reputable financial advisors. If your employer has a financial management program through its retirement program (most do these days), then check it out.
2. Make contact with and interview these individuals to determine if they will be a good fit for you and then select one to work with.
3. Read, read, read books and resources on money management.
4. Be prepared to start saving money. Start small and gradually give your retirement savings a raise. Take a local class or online course on the basics of retirement and personal finance if you are personal finance novice.
5. Establish a budget and follow it. Discipline yourself to

stick to your budget. If you can't establish self-control over your finances, you'll find it very difficult (if not impossible) to accomplish your goals.

6. Stay abreast of the progress with your finances and with your financial advisor. Become a student of money management.

7. Talk to others you care about and love about their money management behaviors. If you don't, you might find yourself taking care of them in your retirement—is that part of your plan?

Your life's goals should lead you professionally and include your retirement life. Now we're ready to discuss your career in human resources knowing you have completed a very important step: setting your compass—understanding how your career and financial decisions can lead to a secure future.

Having an idea of what retirement looks like can help determine your career course of action because you'll need to finance your retirement in some way. Does this mean you should seek to ascend to executive HR levels? Not necessarily. I know a number of people who are financially secure and satisfied working in human resources and who have no desire to work at the executive level in any organization. They handle their personal finances well, they know when they want to retire and where, and they are preparing for their future. They love going home every day at 5:00 p.m. and having their evenings and weekends free to spend with family. They are Blackberry-, Facebook-, LinkedIn-, and Twitter-free, and they are happy. Yes, these people do exist. So is success defined by money and status? Only in the movies! Success is defined by you.

Chapter Review

Write your thoughts about your career direction and setting your compass? Had you ever taken these things into consideration? How do you feel? Does it give you a sense of purpose?

How much income and savings could it take to get you to your place of retirement?

Are you willing to make adjustments to your life now to help you prepare for your retirement if needed? If so, name at least 2 or 3:

CHAPTER FOUR

Safety in Wise Counsel

When we turn to one another for counsel, we
reduce the number of our enemies.

—Kahlil Gibran

Seeking Counsel

As you develop your career plan, career assessments and evaluations are useful for helping you narrow your options and get more focus on your career goals. Completing assessments and evaluations is an obvious step in the career-planning process. However, even with an assessment, you need to balance the results of the quantitative instrument you've completed against the qualitative analysis I like to call wise counsel. You can obtain wise counsel from both individuals and groups of individuals. You can also obtain insight through the informational interview process. The usefulness of the information you gather depends on whether you feel you can use the information—now or into the future.

We all need individuals we can speak with who will help us make wise and informed decisions. Talking with someone who can help you compare the outcomes of survey instruments, performance feedback, and other assessments will ensure that you make the best decision about your future in HR. Perhaps, however, what matters is less about which HR role and more about progression in your career. Many of you reading this book will want to explore senior or executive level opportunities in the immediate future, and some should, but there are others who might need additional development or guidance.

How do you know which level is best for you? Which level in HR is the next step? Which HR career path is the best for your next career move? It's a balancing act. On one hand, you'll need to consider your strengths, weaknesses, and areas of HR that interest you and why—meaning what attitudes, skills, traits, and abilities lead you to believe you would be good in this area of HR. On the other hand, you'll need to consider your experience in the area; feedback from those who know you well, have watched you work, and can tell you more about work-life performance; and insight. Insight from those who are or have performed in an area of HR that interests you but for which you have no practical experience can help you determine if that aspect of HR is really what you wish to do. When you begin to evaluate decisions about your career, as a CEO has the governing board is to a CEO, you too should consider the counsel of advisors. Using the results of the HR Area of Concentration Assessment you completed in chapter 2, let's explore how you might leverage those results to shape and direct your career.

> *I don't believe you have to be better than everybody else. I believe you have to be better than you ever thought you could be.*
>
> —Ken Venturi

Informational Interview

Conducting informational interviews is an easy way to determine if an area of HR is one in which you'd like to work. Informational interviews are not just for the recent graduate. Seasoned professionals looking to change jobs, change careers, or expand their knowledge in their existing area of HR need to put that Rolodex (or LinkedIn site) and those networks to good use in this age of self-guided career management. It is still about who you know, not just what you know.

An example of how to leverage those contacts would be to schedule time to speak with more seasoned HR professionals to explore career growth opportunities (informational interview). Use this time to learn more about that area or level of HR work. As you can see, conducting informational interviews is more than about getting a job. It can also be about maintaining a job and even thriving in that job. Most people have probably conducted an informational interview or two as part of their undergraduate coursework requirement, or have been called on as a working professional by an HR student who wanted to hear their HR insider point of view. These kinds of interviews are also beneficial for career changers, emerging HR professionals, or students seeking a career major.

Here are some reminders:

- Informational interviews are *not* HR interviews. They do not require you to sell yourself to an employer. Remember you're there for insider information about the role *they* currently hold or for which they have responsibility or oversight for in the field of HR.

- Remember this is also an opportunity for you to determine if a particular type of company or organization would be a cultural fit for you. Some people thrive more in not-for-profit organizations than for-profit organizations and vice versa. You'll need to ask about the culture of the type of organization as well as the role within the organization.
- Establish that you will maintain confidentiality about the insights they will share. Agree to not blog, post, write, or otherwise disclose the details of the conversation that will take place.
- If the person you're meeting with did not come from your personal contacts, seek to establish them as a contact in the future. Although this is not an interview, you should follow up as if it were, including a thank-you note. You never know who they might know or what openings might present themselves down the line.
- Informational interviews are not just for new entrants to the workforce and unemployed career changers. You'd be surprised at the number of people opting for career change within the HR field.
- Ask for at least one hour for the interview.
- Make sure you've researched the company and the person you're interviewing, and have some questions prepared to ask.
- Be on time, dress professionally, and end on time.

Questions You Could Ask:

1. How did you get started in this area of human resources? Discuss your career path and how you arrived at where you are today.
2. Do you hold any certifications?
3. What do you think about certification?
4. What was your education and career path?
5. How would you describe a typical day in this job? What skills and ability do you find imperative for success in this job?
6. What are the biggest challenges you face in this role and in this type of organization?
7. What type of things do you read? How do you manage your professional development?
8. Are there resources you'd recommend that I read and add to my library that can help me prepare to work in this type of HR role?
9. If I wanted to work at your level in an organization like this, what type of work/life balance could I expect to have?
10. Why did you choose to work in this area of human resources? Do you think this is where you will continue your career path?
11. Where can this path lead my HR career?
12. What income expectations should I have about this role in human resources?
13. Given recessionary experiences, is this human resource role more or less negatively impacted by the economy?
14. When you think about this industry, what trends do

you see affecting the industry now and into the next 3
years or more?

15. Based on my résumé, how suited am I to this type or
level of human resource work?

16. How can my experiences in non-HR-type roles transfer into an HR role?

17. What are the most important skills, abilities, education, and experiences that factor into a favorable hire
for someone seeking this type of human resource role?

18. What other advice do you have for me?

Finding a Mentor or Coach

Often we use these terms interchangeably to describe a
person or persons who provide us with personal or professional career-related advice, but they are actually quite different. The differences are the period being covered for the
interaction, the intensity, and the amount of time during
each interaction.

If you are seeking a mentor, you are seeking a person
who is in the same type of career field you are in or who is
similarly situated with a greater degree of experience from
which to offer you professional advice. Usually, the mentor
is more senior in age as well as years of professional, career-related, or organizational experience. A mentor is not
always a person you work with or in the same company
but can be a total stranger with whom you consult for a
given period. Most mentor/mentee relationships have an
invisible time table associated with the relationship. Some
evolve into friendships, and others dissipate because the
need for the mentoring no longer exists, or the mentee has

grown out of the need for the level of advice once given.

Mentors can also help you with critical business and career-related decisions. If you are a junior executive or new to the line of work, you should seek a mentor to help you *when* you need to make tough decisions or to think through business processes that may be unfamiliar to you. While you would still be held accountable for the final decision you make, a mentor can offer you the solace of hearing from a more experienced person in your line of work.

If you're not in your chosen career field or line of work just yet, but you have an idea of what you want to do, you can seek a mentor who is doing that very same thing at a higher level. If you just don't know what you want to become when you grow up, then seek wise counsel or a mentor who might be a retired professional in your church or synagogue, a family friend, or another person you look up to. Just being able to discuss your future with someone more seasoned can help guide you through your next steps.

A good mentor will help you think through decisions, not make the decisions or do the work for you. Good mentors will also not try to turn you into mini versions of themselves. I recall a person mentoring me while in my early 20s who told me that to be taken more seriously, I needed to cut my hair and wear fake glasses. Nothing about my actual behavior was ever brought into the discussion. I decided this was not a mentor I needed, never cut my hair nor picked up a pair of fake glasses, and sought the counsel of others for professional advice and counsel instead. Anyone who talks more about him- or herself and less about you and your development is probably not focused on helping you. You may go through a mentor or two before you find one who could actually be helpful. Don't be afraid to keep looking. Never settle on anyone, even if they do have a nice title and are reputable in the community.

A coach, on the other hand, is a person who provides specific instruction and support. A tennis coach offers instruction in the game of tennis; a vocal coach provides instruction for improved singing techniques; and professional business coaches provide guidance for a specific development purpose. A coach should be certified and hold a related degree with some years of experience. As a former human resource executive, I've used business coaches to help guide individuals through challenging on-the-job situations and to help them develop specific leadership behaviors.

A coach is typically brought in to address a specific behavior-related need or challenge. As such, a coach must typically observe a behavior in order to offer feedback. A mentor, in contrast, may never actually see you in action, but rather offer guidance after hearing your description of the situation. My best experiences using coaches professionally were when they offered me feedback after first observing my behavior and entering into dialogue with me and others.

We need both mentors and coaches from time to time. In addition to the examples above on finding a mentor, if you are a current student, you can speak to your college or university academic advisor for recommendations. Otherwise your Human Resources Department may have established protocols to help you in this area. Your local business association may also be a good resource for finding a mentor. Don't count out group mentoring programs or opportunities.

Depending on the individual you select, he or she may have a full plate of mentees and thus invite you to join the small group. This could be extremely beneficial to your career development and relationship management goals.

Still having trouble identifying a mentor? Reflect on the names and faces you've encountered recently that most impressed you. Were they conference or session speakers? Did you read about them in the local print or digital media? Make a list of who's who in your local area among those doing the type of work you would ultimately like to be doing and consider approaching them as well. It is always good to have a list of potentials, because with the time constraints of balancing work and family, some may be better suited and prepared to provide you with support and guidance than others.

For a professional coach, it is important to first grasp what areas of your professional skills or behaviors need development. You'll have a really good sense of those areas upon completion of this book. Once you know where you need development, you should again consider your current employer for any type of career development support they can offer. Unlike the less expensive endeavor of engaging a mentor, sometimes a professional coach requires significant financial expenditures. These licensed and/or credentialed individuals stake their reputation and future business opportunities on being able to help you improve in the areas needed. If you've been instructed or advised that you could use a coach for further career advancement, I implore you to take that advice seriously. Coaching is not a panacea for all behavioral issues, but if you want to ensure that you are not categorized some day as an ineffective leader, you will want to take coaching very seriously.

Coaching, as a profession, has broadened extensively over the years. There are life coaches, professional coaches, and various domains of coaching. To discover the proper way to identify and select the right coach for you, check out these websites:

> www.certifiedcareercoaches.com
> www.coachfederation.org

Establishing Your Personal Board of Directors

I was in a meeting once where one of the attendees referred to his professional network as his personal board of directors (BOD), a group of people at his level (he was a CHRO) who gather to discuss topics of interest to him and his peer group. Noted author, speaker, and networking guru George Fraser states, "At some point in your life, your relationships will become more important than your education." If this is true, then most of us have some work to do.

According to the January 2007 *Harvard Business Review*, there are 3 types of networking: operational, where you network with people in the same organization for work purposes; personal, where you network for personal and professional development; and strategic, where you network inside and outside the firm to better understand and appreciate strategic issues, trends, environmental opportunities and threats, and so on. Most of us have never thought of networking in this way; perhaps we need to take a second look at how we cultivate and build relationships.

Regardless of what you call your group or how you organize your network, as a developing leader in human resources, it is imperative to connect with groups of people

- who are skilled in different functional areas of business (internally and/or externally) and are willing to provide advice and counsel to you and to one another; and
- who work externally in human resources at the same career level with whom you can engage and exchange ideas and information.

For example, if you are a generalist in HR, one network might be with other HR generalists in like organizations at your level. Another network might then be with individuals outside of your own organization who work in different areas of HR, such as benefits, compensation, or employee relations, for example, at or above your career level. And still another variation to your network might be to explore engaging professionals who work in different business areas (finance, marketing, IT) within your organization or outside your organization.

The successful networkers I know, the ones receiving tons of referrals and feeling truly happy about themselves, continually put the other person's needs ahead of their own.

—Bob Burg

I've had iterations of these types of networks at varying times throughout my career. Certain career and professional demands dictated which group or groups were best for that time in my professional life. Do not go out and create or join a bunch of groups just for the sake of doing so. Think through your immediate career needs and then decide which type of group is best for you.

With each of these groups, you can help one another remain current in news and information affecting your career, your line of business, and your organization. HR professionals must broaden their network beyond other HR professionals in their organizational nucleus, and beyond their college graduating class. When you establish and maintain professional relationships with individuals in other lines of business and with different areas of focus, not only do you benefit from the information exchanged but networking enables you to:

1. build on your interpersonal communication skills and your reputation outside work
2. build your confidence and self-esteem
3. be exposed to hidden career and business opportunities
4. test ideas and concepts with a trusted audience of advisors with little to no financial investment
5. generate a database of great ideas for use personally or professionally
6. establish your own word-of-mouth marketing network should you decide to become an entrepreneur
7. generate career, product, and service leads personally and professionally

Where do you start? You can invite friends or people you currently or formerly worked with, or tap into your LinkedIn or Facebook groups, and don't forget your Twitter followers, for both HR and non-HR professionals. Limit the size of the in-person network to a manageable number of 4 or 5, and ensure that you convey the value proposition for them: that they too benefit from this expansion of their network. For virtual networks, your size will obviously be much larger. Organize monthly or quarterly breakfast, lunch, or dinner meetings for your in-person network. Regularly send notes and start discussions with your virtual network.

Chapter Review

Whom might you consider inviting to your professional board of directors?

Operational

Professional

Strategic

What would be the benefit to them?

Operational

Professional

Strategic

What kinds of meetings would you host? Con call, webchat, in person?

How often would you seek to connect?

What is your timeline for establishing your BOD?

Do you have a mentor you can rely on and connect with regularly? What are the benefits, and how might the interaction be more beneficial in the future?

If you do not have a mentor, make a short list of those you might consider asking.

CHAPTER FIVE

The 21st Century HR Professional

Nobody can go back and start a new beginning,
but anyone can start today and make
a new ending.

—Maria Robinson

The Modern HR Professional

What exactly does it take to be considered a 21st century HR professional? Some might say that it obviously depends on the organizational environment and the business expectations of the company you work for. Some organizations are clearly more progressive than others, so a leading-edge 21st century HR professional in one organization might look vastly different from another and both still be considered progressive and successful in their own right.

This is actually not a bad argument because it is true that no two organizations ever operate exactly alike. Even in organizations with multiple locations, though there might be an affiliation agreement holding them together—such as the American Red Cross, Girl Scouts, Heart Association, or franchise operations like McDonalds or Subway—and they might essentially do the same thing, the culture and your experience working in that organization (even the customer experience) will likely yield you a different experience at each location.

To strengthen this argument I'd offer the insight that every successful business or organization *must* take into account the external realities that ultimately influence business success both locally and globally. Relying on skill set, local culture, and local organization or business climate and expectations alone are only the elements of a really good employment advertisement; they do not a progressive HR professional make today. Today's HR professional must therefore:

- be innovative
- be a person of influence
- create win-win outcomes

Innovation

At the heart of a leading HR professional in the 21st century is a muscle that pumps innovation. This truth, and supportive information found by just scanning headlines, points to a world where the HR professional must be able to keep up with and redefine the HR role; as the world changes, business is affected, and HR must strengthen its tentacles to help ensure company success. If the company is progressive and HR is not, then the company suffers. Therefore, an innovative HR professional must establish and maintain a portfolio-exemplified innovation.

Being innovative means taking something that exists and making it different and better or introducing something entirely new. Innovation in HR can come in many forms. It can be new to the organization or new altogether. You could take an existing program and enhance it in ways that help others obtain a different perspective.

Let's take for example the performance appraisal program. The concept is as old as the profession itself; however, it could benefit from sparks of innovation. Performers need feedback to know if they are headed in the right direction or if they need a course correction, and supervisors and leaders need to have a mechanism for providing that feedback. This part of leading is probably the most painful because some people are just not good at confrontational types of interaction. Who relishes sitting in the judgment seat doling out both subjective and objective feedback repeatedly? Well, some do, but never mind them. This aspect of leading is one of the most undesired responsibilities. How can HR be innovative in this organizational tradition, with all of our rules, regulations, and policies? Start by asking "why" and "what" and "what if" questions:

> *Innovation distinguishes between a leader and a follower.*
>
> —Steve Jobs

Goal: A streamlined process for measuring and communicating performance.

- Why is this important for our organization, for our supervisors, for our employees?
- Why do supervisors dislike administering performance feedback?
- What do employees think about the program?

- What suggestions do supervisors and employees have to make it better?
- What if we eliminated the formality of the program and turned feedback into weekly, monthly, and/or quarterly discussions?
- What if the job description were the guide for those discussions? What changes or enhancements to the job description would need to be made?
- What if performance feedback touched on just 3–5 major points?—what is working well, what is not working well, what you need to do to improve in underperforming areas, how your work contributes to organizational success, and in what ways we can enhance the work to achieve greater personal and professional satisfaction and achieve business goals.
- What if documentation were a one-page summary, and what if the meeting were 30 minutes?

This list is not exhaustive, is it? The key here is to keep asking questions until you get to the point where you have something worth exploring further. Sometimes we do things just because that is the way they've always been done. Well, who says we have to keep doing them this way? We don't want change for change's sake, but the best innovations solve a problem or organizational challenge. What challenges does your HR program or organization face? Are their inefficiencies or redundancies, or practices that could use a refresh to save time, reduce expenses, improve employee engagement and satisfaction? Innovation doesn't come easy— take a look around. How might your HR program benefit from innovation?

The 21ˢᵗ Century HR Model

A CEO looking for an HR professional to head up human resources today should look for a portfolio that contains at least these elements:

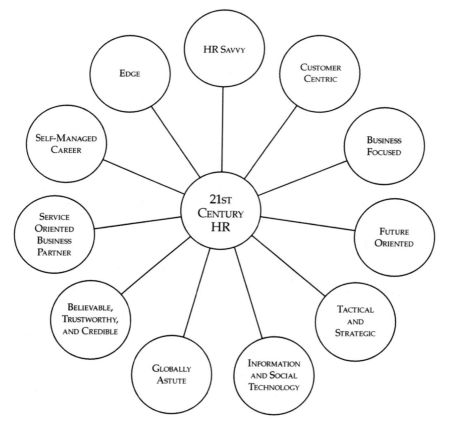

A CEO can't very well know everything, and in acknowledging this, smart CEOs will surround themselves with leaders who will help achieve organizational goals, which makes the HR role critically important. HR, then, as a team must help the CEO locate and assess where the talent gaps are throughout the organization, which requires us to both understand and be intimately involved in the work of the organization. Therefore, being fully engaged in the functionality of the business model, the impact of internal and external realities on the business, strong cross-functional and multi-level relationships require us to remain in perpetual process-improvement mode. Otherwise the company becomes vulnerable to its competitors for talent, market share, and wallet share. Let's explore these elements further:

> **HR Savvy:** Fully comprehends the human resource profession as acquired through a combination of human resource-specific education and work experience, consistently staying abreast of human resource trends, professional changes, and applicable laws, rules, and regulations as well as distinctly differentiating its various applications in the work environment when needed.

With so much talk about obtaining a seat at the table, we've forgotten that a key element of success at the table is *being* an HR professional. You don't have to give up being an HR professional, and doing that well, to be viewed as making a strategic contribution. We wear multiple hats and need a basket full of competencies, skills, and abilities to complement our HR knowledge and experience as we work with others in the organization; but we're at the table not just because we can talk the lingo, but because organizations need someone who can make a direct link between the expected business outcomes and the human capital. When that link is broken or missing, the organization is at risk. There are multiple seats around many tables in most organizations, and each table needs at least one person who is focused on the people employed by the organization both strategically and operationally. Let that person be you.

Customer Centric: Focuses on and understands the changing needs of the customer and ensures that the organization fosters a customer-centric culture.

The customer is both the business employee and the individual who buys your goods or services. HR professionals add value when they understand the needs and behaviors of those they *have* as customers and those they *want* as customers.

A few years back, I was walking through one of the Limited Brand's offices in Columbus, Ohio, with my mentor at the time. I was blown away by a life-size display depicting the customer. That display was a visual illustration of the targeted and average customer of this particular Limited Brand. I will never forget the impact it made on me. It was at that moment that I realized why I loved HR. Only an HR professional could have the brilliance to take the data they had on their target audience and their most valued customer and created a visual that employees would have embedded in their minds, an image that no amount of data could ever accomplish. I still recall the way the person lived, the food they ate, their beverage of choice, their age and gender, how their apartment might look, and what they watched on television. To say it had an impact is an understatement.

When I inquired about the display, I was pointed to the position of the display in the organization and was told that not only was it important for HR to *know* whom they served by reading the various profiles and reports, but that they needed to have a visual and *see* whom they serve. To this end, the display was positioned in such a way that staff had to pass it at least twice daily: going to their office or work area and leaving their office or work area. The visual impression, he said, was a constant reminder of the people they served. He said this affected their internal customer service because they understood collectively the needs of the external customer, and in knowing this, they were able to be more effective business partners, which ultimately affects the bottom line.

Business Focused: Understands the needs of the business and industry and makes the appropriate connection to HR.

The easiest way to build competence in this area of focus is to have dialogue about the business with other disciplines, yes, but also within the HR department. Obviously if you are working as a solo practitioner, your dialogue about the business will be with other peers or leaders in the organization. If, however, you have even just one other person working with you in HR, together you can build your ability to be more business focused:

- Focus your team meetings (even with two people you should have team meetings) around the time immediately following financial postings, staff, and leadership meetings.
- If you are the department lead, you should regularly involve or have conversations with your team about the financials and related HR implications when forecasting and when establishing budgets and making

budget allocations and reconciliations. If you are not the department lead, seek involvement and understanding during your 1:1 meetings with your immediate supervisor and ask for greater involvement in budgeting and planning when possible.

- Read the annual report and other business reports published by the organization.
- Take a business course in the area of business in which you need the most development.
- Subscribe to business magazines such as *Forbes, Harvard Business Review,* or *Black Enterprise Magazine.*
- Check out online resources such as Barron's http://www.barrons.com; Hispanic Business http://www.hispanicbusiness.com; Wall Street Journal; http://wsj.com; and Bloomberg http://www.bloomberg.com
- Conduct and maintain a competitive analysis of your organization's competitors for talent and product or service line and share your findings with key internal stakeholders.
- Pick a business unit for which you have little knowledge or exposure and work with them to solve a business challenge.

All of these and more are ways to enhance your business knowledge.

Future Oriented: Has an eye toward the future and implications for the business and the HR organization. Demonstrates the ability to establish plans to meet implied projections.

The nature of HR is for us to be reactive. Others rely on us to be able to respond quickly, with effectiveness and efficiency, when situations occur. Sometimes we see the issue coming, and sometimes we do not. Regardless, we still have to be level headed in our response and able to offer a satisfactory solution.

This natural role is like being the resident firefighter for the organization, capable of responding to just about any possible emergency situation. The future-oriented HR professional can take these experiences and help the organization plan and create strategy to help mitigate potential human capital and their related business challenges. If I know, for example, that there could be a labor shortage in a critical talent area, as a future-oriented HR professional, I can help my company figure out and even design strategy to mitigate that risk to our business. Another example involves risk and knowing the potential threats to the organization's success, ensuring that the human capital element of risk is adequately addressed among various scenarios.

> *Even if you fall on your face, you're still moving forward.*
> —Victor Kiam

Tactically and Strategically Capable: Understands the difference between being tactical and being strategic. Can adjust performance and interaction to play each role interchangeably when needed. Can quickly distinguish when they need to act in either role.

Research by Lawler and Mohrman (2003) indicates that less than one-fourth of HR's time is spent on the strategic role and that the administrative role decreased only slightly in the survey period. This is not an indictment against HR, because IT, finance, and marketing are just a few of our counterparts who also want to spend more time on strategic initiatives.

Because of the broad implications and potential long-term benefits of implementing a strategic initiative properly, to say you are working on or primarily responsible for some overall strategic activity is sexy, heady, and impressive. However, we can't stay in the clouds all the time. At some point the work has to get done. Being able to differentiate when you need to get involved in tactical operational activities and when you don't keeps your feet grounded and helps ensure that the strategies you put in place are not considered baseless but instead are logical, credible, and conceivable.

An HR professional too focused on strategy will come across as lacking patience for the daily details, or may over-complicate plans (Lominger 2000). On the other hand, being too focused on the details means you may not be able to make the connection to broader significant organizational goals and could likely interfere with routine operational activities. The interplay between being strategic and tactical is critical for any business leader, but especially for the HR professional.

Adept in Information and Social Technology: Being adequately attuned to technological advances that affect the work world and using technology to achieve organizational success. Staying on top of and incorporating social media strategies whenever appropriate.

Today, HR must ensure that all aspects of the business are considering ways to use technology to enhance business processes with positive financial rewards. This is best achieved when HR works with its business counterparts to learn how they use technology and how the use of technology can or has enhanced business. Staying abreast of technological advances affecting the business and making the case for change or improvement will be important for today's HR professional.

It is less about being a tech geek and more about asking the right questions. When there is a business challenge, ask, "Is there a technological solution to this problem?" or "How can we use technology to address these business needs?" About all areas, ask, "What are the latest advances in technology related to this area that can boost our revenue or reduce top-line expenses?" Finally, related to innovation and customer service, ask, "Is there a way to use technology to improve customer service or create a new product line?" These are just a few of the questions HR professionals should be asking in their organizations.

When it comes to social technology, explore, embrace, and acknowledge that it is here to stay. HR should be an early adopter of social technology, not because you want to spy on what your employees are doing, but because your competition is using it to stay ahead of the game. If you aren't allowing employees to blog, tweet, or link in, well, that is just sad. Figure out a way to engage employees and let them be your voice. If you're afraid they'll say the wrong thing, first check out what they are saying in Vault.com and Glassdoor.com—then do what we do best, put some parameters on how employees should use the technology.

A terrific way to engage employees is to create a social technology users' group at work and allow employees to talk about and even test what's new. Allowing and encouraging them to be your eyes and ears in the social technology world will not only save you time, it will help you quickly explore if there is a potential business need for what's hot.

A word of caution: never let technology replace in-person interaction and connection. People will always need to connect face-to-face. Technology is just another way to connect, not the only way.

> **Globally Astute:** Being aware of global challenges affecting the world of work and conveying an understanding of how globalization affects HR.

You don't have to travel globally to be globally astute, though it does help. If your company has offices in other countries, it goes unsaid that you need to be familiar with international employment law. But keeping up with world's social and business news is also important, especially if you have staff who travel globally or have offices in other parts of the world. Ensuring that when you have global visitors, staff are educated on global customs and prepared to interact effectively with your guests is a key role for HR. Also, helping employees who travel globally for business prepare for their trip abroad and their return home appropriately will ensure smooth transition and prevent extreme culture shock.

Another aspect of being globally astute is to create opportunities for high performers and high-potential employees to get exposure to global operations whenever possible. Giving these high performers and high-potential employees exposure to new experiences will extend the life of their engagement with you as their employer of choice. Even if you are working in HR in a domestic U.S. business with no global ties or interactions, you should still ensure that you are conversant in the affairs of this world and the impact on U.S. business. You should know that the future talent shortage will be exacerbated by increasing global opportunities for employment; that foreign colleges and universities are recruiting U.S. college sophomores to finish their senior year in school abroad and then to remain there upon graduation to fuel their talent pipeline; and that with increased globalization comes the need to understand the diverse needs of the workforce.

Believable, Trustworthy, and Credible: Establishing and maintaining an HR culture of trust and credibility. HR in this person's organization seeks to exceed expectations of the internal customer and supports the philosophy of exceptional internal customer focus and service.

The web is filled with HR horror stories, jokes, blog posts, and Internet and magazine articles about bad HR. It is quite sad, but most of it is quite true. Yes, there are really bad HR professionals out there, but that is not who you are. You will be forced to overturn the indictment against HR in many an organization in your career lifespan, and the best way to do that is to

- Do what you say you're going to do.
- Follow up with people in a timely manner.
- Establish a mindset and a culture of customer service in HR (this means HR's service to others and not the other way around)
- Keep confidences.
- Make commitments and establish polices that will benefit others.
- Build a reputation for doing the right thing.
- Weed out the poor performers.
- Excel at communication both in speaking and in writing.
- Come out of your office and talk with people.
- Keep a gallon jar of candy (the good stuff) in the middle of the department—it says "Come in, we're open!"

Business Partners Who Are Service Oriented: Seeking to establish a repeat customer philosophy, such that internal customers readily seek HR's input in key business decisions. Demonstrating and conveying an understanding of both HR and the business to create viable business solutions.

Relationship, relationship, relationship. If you aren't building positive relationships with your counterparts and business leaders in the organization, then how will they know what you can do for them and how you can work together to achieve organizational goals? This is about your relationship with your internal customers and their relationship with your external customers. There are direct links in these relationships, and HR must have the bench strength to make and establish these connections.

Self-Managed Career-wise: Taking responsibility for their own career. Knowing what they like, where they are strong, and areas for improvement. Readily taking on assignments that challenge their knowledge base and establishing career benchmarks they monitor.

Picking up this book is a tremendous step in this direction. Don't wait on your employer to notice you to get that promotion or great job assignment. Set yourself up for success by applying the principles in this book, developing your strengths, and improving your weaknesses. Then you'll be better positioned and have the confidence you need to ask for the promotion or special job assignment. Every year, set a new bar, higher than the year before, and aim to demonstrate concrete evidence of your contribution to the profession. In what way will your employer, your HR department, or the professional be better because you were an active and engaged HR professional? What legacy in HR do you plan to leave? Take responsibility for you, chart your course, and finish your race!

Courageous: Having an edge. The Willing to take on assignments, try new strategies, and test concepts that the average person in their position might not. Capable of standing on their own in the face of opposition and possessing a sense of fearlessness that gets them noticed and respected. Maintaining composure and being unflappable when faced with setbacks or defeat.

Having that edge is both the toughest and the easiest skill to achieve. Remember the Nike tagline "Just Do It"? if edge had a tagline, this would be it. Sometimes you just have to try something new. Face your fears and just do it. I heard a speaker once say that most people come close to crossing the line to success and never cross over for fear of success. Yeah, we blame it on timing, on a "feeling" that something isn't right, but in truth, if we wait for everything to line up perfectly, we'd never do anything. Sometimes picturing the worst thing that could happen helps you move forward, and sometimes it sets you back.

I recall wanting to test a new program in an organization early in my HR career. I had participated in a similar program and wanted to adopt and adapt it to our organization for employee engagement. It required money, time, and trust. It require people to rearrange their schedules, and that I work late nights, early mornings, and weekends to engage even the nursing staff who worked those graveyard shifts.

The risk for me was loss of credibility, that it wouldn't be well received, and that employees would be less engaged, not more engaged. In the end, it was a smash hit! We repeated the training with all staff and annually thereafter until I left the organization. Employee engagement and satisfaction went through the roof! It was a huge risk, but in the end it paid off.

What have you been thinking about that you'd like to try in your company? Is there a new concept you'd like to test? An activity you'd like to try? A program you'd like to launch? If you're afraid of being defeated, then play it out in your head and think of every possible argument against what you're trying to do and then answer the argument. In the end, just say, "I know this is new and maybe even challenging to grasp, but I'm asking you to allow me to give it a try. Will you support me?" If you can stand in the face of opposition, maintain composure, and keep on moving forward, you're well ahead of the game.

Which of the skills above are your towering strengths as an HR professional? Why?

Which two will you need to work on?

A Person of Influence

If you've been in HR for any length of time, you have probably heard of the "seat at the table" conversation that notoriously plagues our profession. As much as I'd like to let go of the reference, the truth is that not only are HR professionals looking for a seat at the table, but anyone seeking to be influential in their organization and in their career is looking for a seat. The C suite seat is not the only seat in town, and HR professionals are not the only ones seeking positions of influence.

In early 2011 I conducted a LinkedIn poll asking if HR professionals were tired of the "seat at the table" discussion. Overwhelmingly the answer was YES. It makes us look wimpy and needy as professionals. As professionals, we are tired of talking about "it." But the truth is, people still want to know the answer. The question simply needs to change from "How do I get a seat at the table?" to "How do I become a person of influence?"

Your HR Influence Guide

> *Even when we're standing still, we often feel the need for a compass, a map or at least some good signposts to help us get moving, see what's up ahead, and understand where we're going. Sometimes we even need a tow, to pull us out of a rut and get us back on the road again.*

—Kelly Mooney, *The 10 Demandments*

What's driving you?

Where do you draw your motivation from? Motivated and influential people often have something driving them.

Sometimes it is their life goals and the drive toward achievement to some expected end, and their career is just a cog in the wheel that is getting them there. To others, their values and belief system not only sustain them but provide them with the spiritual guidance to persevere even in their most challenging times. There are those who have had significant hurt and pain in their lives, and this became the catalyst for their drive to success. For some, their children, a loved one, or a friend inspires them to succeed. Still others find that those micro-accomplishments, like weight loss, smoking cessation, and buying their first home, fuel their drive for success.

Whatever it is, identify and recognize it as your lodestar and constant reminder to stay focused, no matter what tough times you may encounter along the way. If you don't have a source of motivation, take some time to find something that can help you stay motivated and focused. Even tough times can be strange but very effective motivators. Hardship can make you finish a project, find a new job, start a business, finish school, get out of debt, and so on, just to move you from where you are to a much better place—so don't discount the tough stuff.

Describe below who or what is driving you to success and why.

Who are you influencing?

Observing all that drive in you are people who see *you* as their lodestar, even if they never real this to you. Everything you say and everything you do is being observed both intentionally and unintentionally. Some people will seek to observe and report only on the negative things they see and interpret in your behavior. These people would never admit that even they are being influenced by you; subliminally maybe, but nevertheless, you are influencing them. When you challenge people to think differently about a person, place, thing, situation, problem, or opportunity, you are in essence saying to them (in their minds) that what they currently think is not correct. It's human nature to not want to admit when we are wrong, so these people would rather challenge you than readily change their own minds. It is that simple and that true.

If more people would acknowledge that to get something new, they have to change the way they think, we'd probably be building that Tower of Babel talked about in the book of Genesis. Don't let someone's critique of you eat you alive. It is just another form of feedback, and actually a compliment because they are really saying, "You are challenging me to think differently, and I don't like it." You can't possibly please everyone, and not everyone is going to love you, but you can seek to establish and maintain a relationship that allows you to influence their behavior. How do you do this? Well, not by arm wrestling people into submission. You do it by speaking the truth in love, not getting overwhelmed by negativity, picking your battles carefully, holding your position in the face of opposition, and seeking to create win-win situations whenever possible.

Which individuals do you think you are positively influencing?

What individuals in your organization do you want to see you as a person of influence? How might you go about establishing that relationship?

Can you think of ways in which you might be a negative influence? In what ways can you make a course correction?

What influences where and how far you can go?

You picked up this book because either someone said "Here, read this" or you have some desire burning in you to achieve success in human resources. Throughout this book, you will discover what it takes to have a successful career in HR and chart your own path to success; however, it doesn't matter how perfect a plan you write for yourself if you aren't willing to make some type of adjustment in your conduct, your attitude, and your behavior (CAB) to enjoy that success. Your CAB is the vehicle you'll ride (pardon the pun) into success.

Riding in your CAB is your reputation, professional capabilities, work experience, demeanor, expression of thought, physical and mental posture, and likeability. No one loads these into your CAB but you. You control all these things, and no one but you is responsible for how your CAB looks when it pulls up to the door of your job every day. Want to influence your altitude? Change CABs.

The external factor you face riding in your CAB is not about what you can't control, but about what you can influence. No, you can't control how people think, what they do, or even what they say, but you can influence it. Someone may have some deep-seated reason for disliking you or people like you for reasons beyond your control, but your job is not to change their mind but to put your best foot forward in everything you do. Their observation and interaction with you alone will challenge their thinking, which will eventually change their mind.

These things don't happen overnight. You don't buy a person coffee one day and then, snap, just like that, they like you and want to help you in your career. It takes time for them to repeatedly see consistently positive conduct, attitude, and behavior in you that makes the impact and thus the change. It can take six days, six weeks, six months, or six years for influence to take full effect. Be patient and don't lose hope. Change what you can about what is riding in your CAB and watch how far you can go.

What is riding in your CAB that you believe needs improvement?

What is missing from your CAB?

Who or what's influencing your thinking?
The things we see, read, and hear all influence our thinking. The conversations we hold, the programs we watch, the meetings we are in influence how we think. It is important to capture and recognize what influences our thinking because it shows up in our conversation, in our writing, and in our CAB. As professionals, we must be careful to take nutritional sustenance into our minds in the same manner we feed our bodies.

If I want to position myself for leadership opportunities, then I must be cognizant of what leaders expect of someone in the position I seek to obtain. This is similar to the notion of "dressing for the job you want, not the one you have." Feed your mind with positive and productive conversations; seek insight into business decisions. Read related business magazines, and network with progressive people.

Newsflash: people who aren't going anywhere don't want you to go either. You may have to find new lunch buddies if you want to improve your thinking. You'll need people you can converse with to balance and shape your thoughts. We sharpen one another's swords by engaging in conversation. Pick up a book or two on an HR or business topic of interest.

Be careful the environment you choose for it will shape you; be careful the friends you choose for you will become like them.

—W. Clement Stone

Finally, cut out as much mental junk food as possible. Sure, find some time to veg out once or twice a week, but if your daily routine is an 8-hour day at work followed by a long intimate evening in front of the television, you have a lot of opportunity waiting for you. Use your new-found time developing and implementing some of the strategies you're learning about in this journal.

Who negatively influences my thinking? In what ways can I limit my interaction without offending them?

What examples of influencing my thinking above most resonate with me, and which ones can I use to begin making immediate improvement?

WHO/WHAT
IS INFLUENCING YOUR THINKING?
PEERS, FRIENDS, FAMILY,
PROFESSIONAL
NETWORKS,
BOOKS, PERIODICALS,
BLOGS, TV

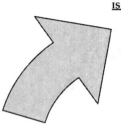

WHO/WHAT
IS GUIDING YOU?
LIFE GOALS
CAREER GOALS
MENTORS
CAREER COACH
VALUES AND BELIEF SYSTEM
MINI ACCOMPLISHMENTS

WHAT INFLUENCES WHERE
YOU CAN GO?
REPUTATION
PROFESSIONAL DEVELOPMENT
WORK EXPERIENCE
ATTITUDE

WHO ARE YOU
INFLUENCING?
DIRECT REPORTS,
LEADERS, PEERS,
CUSTOMERS, CLIENTS,
MENTEES

One of my favorite authors, John C. Maxwell, and co-author Jim Dornan, in their book *Becoming a Person of Influence*, write that influential people possess key characteristics: they have integrity, they nurture other people, they are good listeners, they seek to understand people and help them grow and develop, they help them navigate their personal and career paths, they empower those around them, and they seek to reproduce other influencers. The authors describe stages to becoming a person of influence:

Modeling, becoming the person you want to see in others. People may not remember what you said, but they will remember how you made them feel. What behaviors or qualities are you modeling before others?

Motivating, including connecting with people in a positive way on an emotional level. Helping to build people's self-confidence and positively affecting their self-worth and self-image will lead them to allow you to influence their conduct, attitude, and behavior.

Mentoring is Maxwell and Dornan's third level of influence. Mentoring is a verb, and verbs are an expression of *action*. Thus a mentor is a person who regularly engages in the act of being a wise and trusted teacher and supporter. Mentoring calls for mutual agreement that the relationship is one of teacher and student. Understanding what mentoring is important because many individuals in leadership positions consider themselves mentors to subordinate staff with no correlating action to support their notion of being a mentor. True mentors can track the results of their influence in the life of a mentee; and the mentee can then attest to the influence of the mentor relationship. If you consider yourself a mentor, yet the mentee's life is not being positively affected, improved, and visibly changed by the relationship, I challenge you to consider if you are in fact a mentor or just a friend.

The fourth and final level of being an influencer according to Maxwell and Dornan is the notion of **Multiplying.** These authors contend that in order to attain this highest level of influence, you must "help people they're influencing to become positive influences in the lives of others and pass on not only what they have received from you, but also what they have learned and gleaned on their own." How unselfish and generous one must be to achieve this level of influence.

Creating Win-Win Situations

Creating win-win situations is about how you make people feel, especially in difficult or adversarial situations. As Abraham Lincoln said, "Nearly all men can stand adversity, but if you want to test a man's character, give him power." As an HR professional, you are in the driver's seat most of the time, especially when it comes to decisions about human capital. You have the power to make a situation better or worse. What will you do with that power? Will you use it to benefit someone else, or will you wield it like a giant sling? If we view our jobs as teaching people how to fish, we'll look for teaching opportunities at every turn, instead of handing them a fish called "yes or no."

Say "yes" to new ideas and experiences. I'll never forget the first time I worked in a secretarial role. I had aced all my high school typing and clerical tests and was typing about 100 wpm when I graduated. I knew everything. Then I went to work in an office and was asked to set up some additional files. I looked at the current system. I hadn't seen it before, so I knew it was wrong and decided I would do things "right." After all, it was the 80s—this system must have been outdated. Wrong. I hadn't seen this system for filing because I had never been exposed to it. I didn't ask questions, and when corrected by an office manager, I was somewhat offended. She tried to get me to understand the purpose for setting up the files and folders in that manner, and once I listened, it exposed me to an extremely efficient way of filing.

From there, I looked for new things to learn in every environment. I adopted the mantra that I'd try almost anything at least once. When asked by a different employer to help coordinate a company golf outing, I said yes. I hated the idea of golf and being on a course, but I said yes because I had limited exposure to fundraising. From there I was asked to help with another event, to which I said yes. Did I get extra money, title change, or special acknowledgement? No. But I benefited significantly from the knowledge and experience gained.

In every job situation, learn something new. Learn a new skill, competency, or way of looking at things as a way to build your skill set. In the end, you could find that you're one of the most valued employees in the company.

There *are* situations when a "no" answer is the best answer, and you'll know when those times present themselves. In making your decision, consider:

- Is there a way this offer could help me grow personally or professionally? If so, in what ways?
- Are there any potential setbacks or is there a downside to taking on this responsibility or opportunity?
- How might I leverage this opportunity for my future?
- Am I learning something new?
- Is this moving me in the direction I wish to take my career?
- How will this affect my reputation and credibility?

- How was the decision made to invite me to take on the role or responsibility?
- Is it a temporary or permanent assignment?
- What's in it for me from the point of view from the person extending the offer? (What do they see in me that I might have overlooked?)
- Am I compromising my morals or ethics in any way?
- Is it illegal, harmful, or in any way potentially damaging?

The answers to these and other questions will help you determine if the new opportunity or experience being presented is the right opportunity for you. Keep in mind that not every "offer" is an "opportunity" for you. Assess each situation separately and make a decision that is best for the company but also best for you and your career.

Chapter Review

Assess how close you are to being a modern HR professional.

What items from this chapter most resonate with you?

Have you begun to consider changes you'll need to make to achieve career satisfaction?

CHAPTER SIX

A Mind for Business

Success is not measured by what you accomplish, but by the opposition you have encountered, and the courage with which you have maintained the struggle against overwhelming odds.

—Orison Swett Marden

Business Case

Top business leaders recognize that there are too many options and too many choices available to employees, customers, clients, and consumers in general when it comes to how they spend their time, their money, and their energy. If you want to be in the top class of HR professionals, you must recognize the importance of this key point.

Technological advances are creating new opportunities and introducing more competitors at a rapid rate. These technological advances and rapid growth in direct competition is eating away market share and eating into revenue of businesses across the world. Top business leaders recognize that the buffet of technological advances being made available to consumers means that customer loyalty will come at a premium. This type of competition has sparked the focus on corporate social sustainability and responsibility, growth in customer loyalty programs, and public relations campaigns designed to capture the heart and mind of consumers who increasingly are doing business with those organizations that are socially responsible, who pay attention to their individual needs, and whom they know, respect, and trust.

Let's take a look at something closer to home for HR—the workforce! If according to the Bureau of Labor Statistics, the workforce is shrinking and there will be more jobs than people to fill them, top talent will soon not be as readily available. Contributing to this trend:

- Top college students being actively recruited by colleges and universities in global markets to finish their education abroad and, once complete, stay on a work visa to fill the global talent gap.
- Women and people of color, fed up with the politics and bureaucracy of trying to climb the corporate ladder, are leaving the workforce in large numbers to start their own businesses—many competing against their employers.
- Students and young professionals have their sights set on global opportunities outside of college and are willing to take long-term assignments over their more senior and often more settled counterparts.

The trophy goes to the organizations best able to provide lucrative options to their top performers in the new workforce, options such as global assignments and travel, bonuses, flexible work, training and development, challenging work, great pay and benefits, recognition, and rewards. Top performers are going to cost a premium to recruit and retain. Just like a college football recruiter, in the coming years, if not next year, you too may find yourself in the living room of a high potential candidate, trying to entice him or her to work for your company. Leading-edge business-minded HR professionals recognize the importance of employee engagement and retention today in the wake of a shrinking workforce and are convincing their CEOs to support establishing employee engagement programs and practices that will feed the talent pipeline now and into the future.

Given the two scenarios above, how can you make the case to the CEO of the importance of investing in HR initiatives, especially in the wake of tough economy, declining revenues, and organizational challenges? If your organization does not have a process for implementing new ideas, here is a 5-step process for making the pitch:

Recognize the dilemma

The situation might be crystal clear to you, but CEOs, given a choice, are going to focus on what they believe is most critical and threatening to the business. Who could blame them? If two vehicles are coming toward you, and both pose a threat, you're going to avoid the one likely to have the most damaging effect. CEOs will often see the technology threat as an 18 wheeler driving downhill at 65 MPH, and the workforce threat as a 10-speed bike. The key is to not overexaggerate the threat. Make the issue relevant and don't make the CEO pick. Don't make this an either/or situation. Once you recognize that all the other business disciplines are projecting and forecasting too, your job is to then help him or her see how having the proper talent in place will prevent that 18 wheeler from getting out of control.

Crystallize the business opportunity

Define and articulate the exact problem or challenge facing the organization. Why is it a problem? Is it because of legislative or governmental changes? Has your organization made changes to its strategy? Have there been commercial developments in the marketplace that pose a threat? Is there another employer moving into the area that could siphon talent? When did you recognize it was an issue? What are the implications if not resolved? What is the timeframe for addressing and bringing resolution? How much of an investment and what type of investment will it require? What supportive data can you offer to support your case? This includes financial implications, research, and your own workforce analysis. Also, historical data analysis of your organization's performance (employee surveys, trend analysis, workforce analysis) is a good source for predicting future performance. Spend time at the library—yes, they still exist—with a librarian who will help you identify the resources you'll need to build your case.

Suggest alternative solutions

After crystallizing the opportunity, you'll need to present alternative solutions to your immediate supervisor if not the CEO. There will be a number of solutions you could select; however, your job is now to narrow the number of solutions to those that yield the greatest return. An example of how you might lay it out would be:

Summarize the Business Challenge:

Describe Solutions	Pros	Cons
Solution A		
Solution B		
Solution C		

Ensure you forecast the costs and risks associated with implementation of each solution.

Recommend a preferred solution

The solution you recommend for implementation should be the one you believe will bring about the greatest benefit to the future of the organization. You'll need to define why you are recommending this particular solution. Don't focus on the lowest cost to implement. You want to focus on the greatest return for your investment, and in some cases, it may cost more to get what you are seeking. If these are employee-related costs, speak in terms of investment, not just expense. In your outline of your preferred solution, make sure you address:

- Your implementation timeline and communication strategy

- If there will be a need to establish a project team, who would be asked to serve, the role of the team in the planning process, and expected time commitment

- The measures of success: What does success look like and how will you know it was a success? What measures will you put in place to evaluate progress over time?

Gain buy-in and support

This is the opportunity to work both within and across functions and departments, especially stakeholders, to discuss your idea. This responsibility to obtain buy-in and support may need to come at the genesis of your idea, once research is complete and your are forming your recommendation. In other organizations it may need to come at the end, once you've "sold" the idea to your immediate supervisor if not the CEO. Be cognizant of internal culture and politics when establishing a business case, and respect your culture. Bottom line: if you don't know, just ask.

How Companies Value Their Employees

Ask one hundred or more companies how they value employee performance and you'll get a hundred similar answers: the bottom line, client/customer interaction, and something about your personal or professional contribution to the company—your dedication. Let's sum it up this way: companies value you based on three things—what you know, what you think, and what you do.

You are hired primarily for what you know. You are then evaluated, and your success is determined by what you think and what you do—and sometimes your success depends on what you do about what you think and know. When you learn something new that resonates deep within, sometimes you make a note of it or it becomes burned in your memory such that you can recall it at a moment's notice when the opportunity presents itself. Think about those notes, mental and physical. When was the last time you pulled them out and took action on them? Some of the most successful people find a way to use those salient points of information they learn.

It might not be new information to everyone, but it's what you do with what you know that leads to success. We may never know the name of the guy who invented the Post-it note for 3M, but we know he acted on what he knew might work. He took a risk and acted on his knowledge, and it

Believe in yourself! Have faith in your abilities! Without a humble but reasonable confidence in your own powers you cannot be successful or happy.

—Norman Vincent Peale

paid off only after he acted on it. What thoughts and ideas are you thinking about but not acting on? Are you missing or overlooking a career or business game-changing opportunity?

The genesis therefore lies within you. Success in human resources and HR's success organizationally requires you to constantly feed your intellect and give thought to and shape opinions around how what you know can generate positive return to you professionally and to the organization. Consider:

- Are you regularly reading and feeding your mind with useful information? Are you building and engaging in meaningful discussion with your network? Are you engaging leaders in your organization just to talk about their lines of business and what *they* think and need?
- Do you repeatedly assess your contributions to the HR department and to the organization and make course corrections and improvements as needed?
- Are you contributing to or building a positive image of HR's reputation and credibility in the organization, not because of your position, but because you want to build on the credibility of the organization and your role as a professional?
- Do people trust you enough to come to you for solutions to their people problems and business issues or concerns and trust that you will help them work through their challenges? Or are they going to others about things they've heard because HR is last place they go for help? Are you on the inner circle of the organization's communication chain or the outer loop?

If in a leadership role:

- Are you helping your staff grow and development, weeding out those who are not motivated and are not making a measured and meaningful contribution?
- Are you talking with the CEO about what's on his or her mind, and is the CEO concerned about what is on your mind?
- As the chief culture officer, are you and your leadership satisfied with the culture? If not, are you actively working to improve it?

- Are you learning about the changes in the profession and adjusting yourself and the direction of your team accordingly?

The elephant in the room for HR is this notion of being viewed as strategic. We tend to find that our contribution has to be in our ability to give the answer to the equation rather than to help the seeker find his or her answer. It's the adage that if you give a man to fish, you feed him for a day, but if you teach him to fish, you feed him for a lifetime. HR has to learn that they don't always have to give the answer but can teach others how to find the solutions to their problems.

When grocers started incorporating self-service checkout lines, they weren't trying to avoid critical customer service, but it enabled them to focus their resources on other crucial areas of the business that needed attention. This is how HR professionals must begin to view their roles. Being so needy that business leaders can't make a move without first going through you is like hanging a sign around your neck that says, "I'm insecure in my job and need control over your decisions to make me feel important."

Being an enabling HR professional frees you up to focus on the more strategic areas of HR. It also frees you up to work in areas of interest in HR and to exercise your creativity and invite innovation into the HR department. One of the things I used to do to help free up my time was script supervisors who needed to have disciplinary or coaching conversations with their staff. The first time I'd sit with them and offer them feedback at the conclusion of the session. The second time, I'd give them the script, coach them on things to look out for, and have them go through their performance session alone. They'd then have to report back to me how things went, how they felt, and what things they neglected to cover in the script, just in case I needed to come behind them and clean things up or do damage control. Teaching supervisors how to fish, or deliver disciplinary or coaching conversations, kept me from having to sit in on every single performance discussion, freed up a significant chunk of my time, and made them feel empowered as leaders.

Once you've freed up your time, you can begin thinking about what you want to focus on in the organization. This requires you to think of HR in the context of the business, and to do that you have to know the business. First, among many things, HR thought says:

- Where will my talent come from now and into the future?
- How will I engage and retain top talent?
- How can I effectively deal with poor performers?
- What type of culture does the company want to create?
- How is HR viewed in the organization? What are the benchmarks? How can we improve, establish a standard of excellence, and consistently perform well against that standard?
- What role do external realities play in the world of HR in the organization?
- How can I ensure that leaders have the talents, skills, ability, and attitude to meet organizational needs?
- What systems, processes, and procedures can I put in place to make leadership in our organization exciting, rewarding, and effective?

- What measures can I share to help leaders identify opportunities for growth and improvement?
- What measures can I share to demonstrate HR's value and contribution to the bottom line?
- When was the last time I asked how an HR decision might affect the bottom line? Do I know what that means?
- When was the last time I asked how an HR decision today might affect business in the foreseeable future (or 3–5 years from now)?

Business thought says:

- How do we make money?
- What is our business model?
- What are our key performance indicators?
- When the economy shifts, where do we likely see positive growth or diminishing returns?
- When was the last time we conducted an environmental scan, what did it tell us, what did we learn, and did we make adjustments to the business accordingly? Why or why not?
- Are we regularly discussing external factors affecting business and the world at work and their potential impact to the bottom line?
- What scenario plans are in place and who is monitoring them?
- If I scan the lists of companies that have won awards or are recognized for their business management practices, innovation, financial stability and growth, employee engagement, etc., what things do they have in common? Are we on that list? Why or why not?

- What is our reputation?
- Is the process flow in our organization helping us to become more efficient and effective? Who is monitoring the process flow for our organization? How do the outcomes compare against our forecasts and performance indicators?
- How are workflow interruptions such as absenteeism, silos, mistakes, and rework affecting the business? How do we avoid and prevent these types of interruptions?
- Who are our competitors? Who is keeping an eye on them?

These lists are not exhaustive; however, you can use these questions as starting points to shape your thinking about your company and the work of HR in your company. Being strategic and being viewed as strategic are dependent on the questions you ask and the things you do. Just asking these questions and pontificating publicly about what you think no more lends credibility to you as a leader than to know the reasons for a problem and never speak up to offer the solution. Timing and articulation are critical to being influential in your organization.

Moving forward in your HR career requires a realistic look at your skills, capabilities, and strengths to bring about the greatest job satisfaction, marketability, transfer of skills, and income potential for you and your family. So, where have you been, what have you done, and how well did you perform? Answer the following questions about your employment experiences overall:

1. Professional Marketability

2. My most memorable and fulfilling work assignment to date has been:

3. People I work with tell me I'm really good at:

4. I get the greatest satisfaction at work when I am doing:

5. I would highlight the following skills, strengths, and capabilities to a potential employer:

6. The best company I've ever worked for is _____ because:

7. I feel the company that best took advantage of my strengths was _____, in this way:

8. Looking at my accomplishments, a potential employer would find the following things valuable:

9. I can point to at least 3 significant accomplishments if asked by a potential employer, and they are:

Reflection

This section requires you to take a look at yourself. Taking a deep introspective look inside to examine your motives, your sense of determination, and your willingness to pursue something so important that you will do whatever it takes, even if it means going outside your comfort zone or taking significant risks to make it come to pass.

Many of you reading this book have taken some pretty tough blows to your self-esteem. After enough times getting denied promotions and job offers, or having to put your career on hold, it is so easy to feel beat up on and wallow in it a little. Have you ever looked back on a seemingly missed opportunity only to discover you really didn't miss anything?

For others, this journal is about planning the future. You

may have a job but it isn't ideal nor what you would call a "career." Perhaps you see change coming down the pike and need to plan for it. For you, this journal is your exit strategy.

Regardless of your reason for completing this journal, at the end of the day, what is most important is that you walk away from this experience willing to believe in yourself even against the odds, believing in and improving on your own capabilities and your strengths.

If we are honest with ourselves and rewind the tape, there were probably some opportunities that we could have obtained, but in looking back, we either weren't ready from a skill set, competency, and attitude perspective, or we did not properly assess our readiness to take on the challenge. What did we learn from those experiences? Anything? Or did we shrug it off as "their loss"?

Sometimes in the interview process, we get so focused on how to answer a question, we forget that the interviewers are really giving us insight into and information about the job. They aren't asking you questions just to kill time and play a game. They seriously want to know what you know, how you think and if you can effectively perform the job—all within an hour or so.

> *Most people give up just when they're about to achieve success. They quit on the one yard line. They give up at the last minute of the game, one foot from a winning touchdown.*
>
> —Ross Perot

Every candidate should know if a job is for them based on the questions asked before and during an interview. Listen carefully. What story is the interviewer telling you about the company? What is important to them? Are you demonstrating the ability to meet their needs? If you listened to the exchange of communication throughout the process, you should be able to:

- assess if you spoke the lingo of the field, business, or industry;
- link current affairs to business realities;
- properly assess the culture for your organizational fit.

If you didn't conduct any research on the company prior to exploring a career with them, and if your cover letter and résumé oversold your capabilities—these could have contributed to presumably lost opportunities.

We've all made mistakes and poor decisions. We've all suffered from bad judgment. We are not perfect. The fallacies occur when we make the exact same mistakes over and over and expect different (sometimes better) results.

As you complete this step, give yourself the permission to admit mistakes, learn from your past, and move with determination into your future.

Moving to the Next Level

To take your career to the next level, a critical step is to explore and come to terms with your source of motivation. Change for change's sake without personal purpose and meaning could lead to a life filled with unhappiness. Going to the next level in your HR career may require you to change, take some risks, travel, speak publicly, or develop other skills or competencies. In a global world, the possibilities for you in HR are virtually limitless; however, only you know your limitations. Consider your motivations for moving forward and **check only 3**:

❏ Greater authority or leadership role

❏ Autonomy in my work

❏ Business-related travel

❏ Responsibility for supervising people

❏ No responsibility for supervising people

❏ Opportunity to capitalize on my creativity

❏ More job security (tired of threat of layoff in this line of work)

❏ More money (want to maximize my income potential)

❏ Balance between work and family (overtime is not an option)

❏ Greater prestige and visibility

❏ More of a set daily routine (I like the consistency of knowing what I'll be doing from day to day with minimal change)

❏ Variety of tasks on a regular basis (I like a lot of change)

❏ Team-oriented work

❏ Work from home most days of the week

❏ Flexibility and freedom from a routine work schedule

❏ Other preferences:

If you are ready for the next level, not only must you be willing to expand and change, but you must be able to function well as a good corporate citizen. Think about it: you will be working for someone else until you retire, and most of us who don't plan to stop working until our pulse stops will work for someone until we die. This means you must be able to work successfully in an environment controlled by someone else. Three key areas I call "pulse points" must be mastered by anyone seeking to have a long healthy career doing what he or she loves while working for someone else: people, policy, and politics.

People

Dealing with people effectively is an art. If you want to get anything done in any organization you do not own, you must be able to manage yourself, build relationships with co-workers, deal effectively with senior management, and connect with subordinate staff. All of these people will, at one time or another, hold the key to your success. No one person holds all the cards. You have to work through and with all levels of people all the time. If you're snotty to the mail person, guess whose mail could get held up? If you can't get along with co-workers, who will help you in a pinch? If you aren't demonstrating team and leader capabilities, guess who will get looked over for great projects, fun assignments, or high-profile opportunities? Make sure you are building relationships up, down, and sideways to find success in human resources, regardless of your organization.

Customer management is a critical part of the people equation. For anyone who ever has to deal with a customer, I recommend the book *The 10 Demandments,* by Kelly Mooney. This book is probably one of the best books ever written on customer service. I sent her an e-mail recently applauding the writing and telling her how much I wish she had a little pocket book I could purchase and hand to people who worked in customer service but didn't fully grasp what it meant to *deliver* great customer service. Please *run* to purchase this book if you deal with customers. The 21st century customer is setting the *new* customer service standard,

Consumers are giving their trust, business, and eventual loyalty to the companies that do right by them.
—Kelly Mooney,
The 10 Demandments

and regardless of what business you are in, you have to be customer oriented in an effort to keep up. More businesses today depend on the quality of customer service they deliver to keep them a going concern in the marketplace.

Policy

The second important pulse point is that of policy. What are the company policies and procedures? Are there any policies of particular importance to your career or job function? Some policies, if violated even once, can be career limiting with certain organizations. Some policy violations produce life-threatening situations, and still others can be damaging to the health and safety of you, your co-workers, or the company brand. Pay close attention to the policies that govern your work and your work environment, not only in your company, but also in your field. Having worked in the healthcare field for a major part of my career, I can attest firsthand to the importance of establishing and following proper policies and procedures. Believe it or not, something as simple as not properly washing your hands can cause serious illness to you and to those you care for inside and outside a healthcare environment.

Politics

Finally, let's address politics. *Every* organization has its own brand of politics, even in HR. The degree to which politics affects your daily career routine depends on your individual organization and how the work gets done. Simply, politics is "how" things get done in your organization. Politics is how decisions are made, and it is very important to know that process. Corporate politics are sometimes just as nasty as the politics surrounding our local and federal governments, sometimes nastier. Regardless, it is important to understand how the work gets done, through whom decisions must pass, and which key individuals need to be involved for you to find career success.

Likeability

At the end of the day, promotions are not won, jobs are not offered, and doors are not opened simply because you possess all the skills, education, and experience required for a given job. People want to help people they like *and* who possess all those things. If you can't establish a connection quickly with people, a connection that is genuine and sincere, then you may find it difficult to accomplish many of your career, personal, and interpersonal goals.

Let's be perfectly clear—some people won't like you, as one coach put it to me, "simply because they just don't like you." Most of the time you'll be able to recognize them immediately in how you are treated and in the things they say to you and about you. Only you can determine if the relationship is worth pursuing to raise your likeability rating in their eyes. If, for example, a boss is the one whom you feel doesn't care for you, then that is probably a relationship worth pursuing and improving. If, on the other hand, the person is less significant, you can try to address it, or simply let it go. To pursue everyone whom you feel doesn't like you can become tiring and frustrating. It can also make you appear needy, and in such cases, you lose friends and influence because you are tiring someone else out with all the neediness.

In the book *The Likeability Factor: How to Boost Your L-Factor and Achieve Your Life's Dreams*, Tim Sanders points out that

> Life is a series of popularity contests. The choices other people make about you determine your health, wealth, and happiness. And decades of research prove that people choose who they like. They vote for them, they buy from them, they marry them, and they spend precious time with them.

Not too long ago, my husband and I were in a search of a home in the Maryland, DC, and Virginia areas. If you know anything about this area, you'll know that we had lots of options to choose from. We had a terrific Realtor, who patiently educated us on the area and the housing market on the East Coast. The housing and employment markets in the DC area do not mimic the rest of the country. Even during the recession, the housing market remained relatively stable. Several factors contributed to this, including government and military workers, travel, and tourism. This meant that while there were a lot more homes available for us to choose from, there was an equal number of people also seeking to snatch a great deal.

In the 2.5 years since relocating to the area from Ohio, I had easily seen over 200 homes, some with my realtor and others by doing Internet searches and then drive-bys on my own. By the fall of 2010, my family and I were tired and ready to settle on a home. It is true that there is no perfect home, just as there are no perfect marriages, families, or companies to work for. You will need to find a way to concede to some of the things on your list. After we found the home of our dreams, we met with our Realtor, the broker, and the builder only to discover that someone else wanted to purchase *my* home. While I thought it came down to money and credit worthiness, I discovered during the process that it came down to likeability. The other couple was just as credit worthy as we were. They had a nice family and great jobs too. They completed the paperwork and followed the procedures just as we had done. The deciding factor, we discovered later, was that the builder's broker and staff liked us much better.

How many job opportunities, promotions, and other experiences were you denied simply because you did not connect with the decision makers?

I grew up with a mother and father who used to tout the phrases "You get more bees with honey than with vinegar" and "Attitude determines altitude," and they were so right. Sometimes we make it so easy for people to say "no" or to deny us an opportunity because we approach the situation already defeated or with too much pride and arrogance. Living with these two extreme attitudes is begging for failure. So what can you do? How do you know if your attitude is holding you back? If you are unsure if your attitude is holding you back, you'll certainly obtain feedback about that later in this journal, but consider:

- How well do you get along with others?
- Are you most often sought after for advice or for the latest gossip?
- If you were to conduct a 360-degree survey of everyone you work with—I mean everyone and not just the people you believe will assess you favorably—would the outcome about your attitude be more positive or negative?
- When you think about promotional opportunities, would you want to be led by you? Why or why not?
- Are you more of a peacemaker or a troublemaker?
- Would a survey of your peers and co-workers reveal you were more or less respectful of people? In other words, do you or do you not treat people with actual or perceived higher position, power, authority, or status more favorably than those without power, position, authority, or status?

We know ourselves much better than we let on. In your time of quiet reflection, some soul searching could be life changing. At the end of the day, no matter what you do, it is your attitude that will ultimately determine your future success.

Chapter Review

What's holding you back? What are your personal and professional limitations? How can you work around them to achieve career success?

What areas of business savvy require your focus and attention? Can you pinpoint times when you lose focus? What things can you do to stay on task?

What other areas for improvement might you want to remind yourself to consider as you progress in your career timeline?

CHAPTER SEVEN

Young Professionals in HR

Don't worry when you are not recognized,
but strive to be worthy of recognition.
—Abraham Lincoln

E verything in this journal is applicable to you. I've created this special chapter, however, for my younger HR friends out of my admiration for your enthusiasm and determination and my desire to see you hit the ground running in a race that calls for you to be the ultimate winner—the future business leaders and CEOs of organizations small and large across the world.

Obtaining Your HR Job

Obtaining a job, especially in your career of choice, is extremely exciting. The best chance of obtaining an HR job, or any job today, depends on what you know and how well you are able to demonstrate that in the interview process. What will help you is getting practical hands-on experience, best obtained through internships and volunteer opportunities. Both count toward practical work experience if you are able to actually perform HR work.

Internship and volunteer opportunities are about you making a connection between your college experience and real world application. Learn as much as you can about application of HR, yes, but also about working within organizational cultures, the assimilation process, and how HR work gets done in that particular organization. Journal the good, bad, and ugly HR and cultural experiences. Make note of what you liked about the experience and what you didn't like. What might you do differently, better, or uniquely if you worked as a regular employee? In a leadership position? Make note of those in leadership—what are the most and least admirable behaviors you've observed? What were the written and hidden rules of engagement in the company that gave you the most frustration? What did you learn? Where did you find success and why? How did you compare to others who currently or were previously similarly situated in your role? The answers to these questions and more will prepare you to transition to your job in human resources.

Now the moment of truth. Finally, the theories you studied in college, the strategies you learned and tested during internships and volunteer opportunities, and the concepts you learned in HR conferences and local meetings will have voice in your new HR job. Maybe.

Hitting the ground running for you will require you to make the distinct connection between what you've learned and how you apply what you've learned or what you know. Sometimes it is the common sense behaviors in HR that trip up emerging or young HR professionals:

- Knowing the importance of confidentiality and how to properly safeguard confidential information. Something as simple as keeping confidential paperwork concealed, turning it over when not being used, is critical in this information and identity theft age.

- Clearly understanding work assignments and making no assumptions in completing them.
- Asking questions until you are confident you understand what is expected of you.
- Getting help as soon as you need it.
- Developing a keen understanding of the needs of your internal and external customers, and delivering exceptional customer service at every opportunity.
- Learning the corporate culture, the company's story, and how the company functions and makes money. These are critical to connecting the dots to what you do and how it affects the bottom and top lines (revenue and expense).
- Reading everything you can, including the employee handbook. Yes, you're back in school.
- Being proactive in seeking new assignments or job-enriching opportunities without the consistent expectation that you'll reap financial rewards or other perks—sometimes learning something new *is* the perk and can lead to financial rewards later in your career.
- Making the connections to what you are being asked to do and larger work processes or outcomes.
- Properly developing relationships within the business unit and around the organization at various levels, not just in your age group, demographic group, or job level.
- Obtaining an internal mentor or coach to help you learn the culture or HR "ropes" in your particular organization.

- Applying the strategies conveyed in this journal and remaining committed to your professional development.

This list is not exhaustive, but a more seasoned HR professional reading this book might bookmark this chapter for their younger team members. Truth is, we all need a refresher from time to time. This is part of earning your dues as a young professional.

Keeping Your HR Job

Developing your HR thought process and tying it to job expectations and business outcomes are critical aspects of keeping your HR job.

- Be clear on the expectations of your job. Review your job description with your supervisor when you first start and annually during your performance review discussion.
- Be a student of business and HR.
- Read your favorite HR and business publications
- Apply something you've learned to the work you do to complete the assignment, offer something new to the organization, or enhance an expected outcome.
- Keep track of your accomplishments.
- Develop and maintain good boss and peer relationships.
- Seek professional development at an appropriate pace: trying to do too much too soon could be intimidating to longer tenured employees and thus create unnecessary roadblocks as a result. Also, longer tenured employees may be offered development opportunities ahead of you.

Thriving in Your HR Job

As a young professional, you can flourish in your job, and though weird might be the new norm in popular culture, it may not necessarily be the new norm in the predominately traditional work environment of today. Organizations with "cool" cultures like SAS, Zappos, Abercrombie and Fitch, and others who offer the opportunity to roller blade on campus, wear casual clothing, and so forth, still require you to meet and exceed the requirements of your job. Those who are offered cool assignments, job enrichment opportunities, and promotions are those who *consistently* go above and beyond in their job, and who can work across cultural and organizational barriers. You're facing the experiences of multiple generations at work, from those who firmly believe you need to work to earn your place at the top, and even those who believe young people should be seen and not heard, to you—your generation of faced-paced doers.

You might ask, "How do I do that without seeming to be an overachiever and alienating my peers and others in the organization?" The answer is easier for me to convey than for you to do. At some point, young professionals will have to learn to break away from the pack. Or better that I say wean themselves away from the pack. This doesn't mean abandon your fellow lunch mates, but it does mean broaden your network and organizational exposure. Thriving as an HR professional today is exactly what this journal is about. I won't taunt you by quipping "just finish the book," but instead let me offer some sound advice to my junior super achievers.

As a leader, I can promote only one person at a time. Rarely are multiple promotional opportunities available within a department in short periods. In promotional situations, supervisors are looking for individuals who can, with help, manage the politics of going from peer to supervisor while developing and executing operational and strategic goals. Going from peer to supervisor is best done when you have already established credibility with your peers. Those *not* ready for leadership opportunities tend to exhibit these kinds of behaviors:

- Repeatedly agreeing with and following the decisions of the crowd, even to their own detriment
- As a peer, repeatedly turning to the crowd to help make decisions that affect their own work
- Having a reputation for getting overly involved in water cooler discussions and as a regular contributor to the gossip ring
- Bonding with the less reputable employees at work
- Lacking control of their emotions in situations that affect them or others they care about
- Offering feedback to others or in work scenarios that is perceived as more destructive than constructive

All of these are just some of the ways in which you can be derailed early in your career. Avoiding these situations requires you establish productive and supportive work relationships. Observing and taking note of the way work gets done in your organization and how the more respected and accomplished leaders in your organization find success will be key to how well you thrive. Take note and remain in constant self-improvement mode.

Lastly, adopt an attitude of exceptional customer service. Seek to create win-win scenarios for even the worst customer interaction and respond in a timely fashion and with a good attitude when someone reaches out to you for assistance. People will always remember how you made them feel. In this customer-driven society we live in, the ability to obtain and maintain customer loyalty and engagement (internal and external) will get you noticed.

Dress Code

Many work environments demand a business or business casual dress code. Though a growing number of organizations over the years have adopted an even more casual dress code for their work environments, even within the most casual work environments, several codes are often actually in play: "In a new CareerBuilder.com survey, 41 percent of employers said that people who dress better or more professionally tend to be promoted more often than others in their organization" ("How to Dress for Success at Work," www.cnn.com/2008/LIVING/worklife/07/30/cb.dress.for.success/index.html).

There can be as many different dress codes in an organization as there are departments or divisions. The key will be knowing what is appropriate and being willing to adjust your style based on where you want to go rather than settling on just where you are. Consider your internal and external audience when evaluating how to dress as an HR professional. If you are consistently in business meetings with outside guests or customers, then consider adopting a more business professional dress after you've observed the dress code in your department. It is okay to step it up a bit in adhering to the dress code policy. Working in a casual environment where everyone wears jeans daily doesn't necessarily mean you can't balance between being underdressed and overdressed. Take a look around, observe the style and dress of the more respected and credible peers and supervisors, and adopt their style with your own flair and personality.

Non-negotiables

- Build your professional network by connecting virtually and in person.
- Join a professional association for your HR career and get involved.
- Create and rehearse your "elevator speech" to introduce yourself when networking.
- Become a proficient public speaker or presenter and a good writer. Business writing skills are highly valuable.
- Build your vocabulary, speak the king's English when you need to, and use slang only when it is appropriate outside work.
- Some people just aren't going to like you just because they don't like you. Focus on building relationships on the team and off the team. Don't focus on being a people pleaser so much as a relationship builder.
- Gone are the traditional 8-hour work days. Be mindful of what you say and do virtually and publicly: you represent your company's brand from the moment someone asks you, "Where do you work?"

Leaving Your HR Job

How you leave your job is just as critical as how you start a new job. The HR world is both large and small at the same time. Even if you weren't well connected in the local HR network, it is likely that someone you have worked with is well connected. The purpose for establishing these connections is to gain access to information that might not be otherwise available to the average person. For example, most companies today have policies that prevent offering references, but you really don't believe that there is no way someone can obtain a reference on your past performance, do you? As a young professional, you ought to be building a solid reputation, one of credibility and trust among other things. People are 10 times more likely to communicate negative information than positive. This means one mistake could follow you well into the future. Here's some advice:

- Give notice inside the stated policy. If no policy is given, then offer at least a 2-week notice. If in a leadership role, the rule of thumb is 30 days.
- Communicate in private with your immediate supervisor and then offer a written notice.
- If a counter offer is extended, consider it over a reasonable time frame, a few days, and promptly get back to your employer with your answer. If you decline the offer, send a written letter that acknowledges and thank them for thinking of you in such a way that they would extend a counter offer, explaining that you believe the move you are making is the best one for you at this time in your career.

- Never speak negatively about the employer with co-workers or future employers.
- Stay away from negativity about your past, present, or future employers in social media networks, because as the saying goes, you can't unring a bell.
- Finish pending assignments, ask for guidance for establishing priorities to close out projects, and don't slack off.
- Ask for a written letter of reference from your immediate supervisor and secure it before you leave.
- Leave a letter to your successor helping locate key files and giving insight into the systems and processes you have in place.
- Keep a copy of things you've created or make note of systems and programs you've implemented to add to your career portfolio. It is often impossible to obtain copies once you've left your employer. While you may not be able to claim ownership of intellectual property (resources created for or on the behalf of the employer), you can certainly take credit.

These are just some things that will help you make a proper exit from your current employer when the time comes. Thinking in terms of legacy building in your exit will help you stay focused. Sometimes, leaving is tough, but when the leaving is easy and you can't wait to get out, still adhere to this advice and be thankful you're leaving. Don't give anyone a reason to say something negative about you.

Chapter Review

If working, volunteering, or interning, are you journaling your experiences?

Are you assimilating to the corporate culture—their way of doing things? Make note of what you like and dislike about this company's culture. If the culture concerns you, consider if the issue is the company or if you need to make changes to your own conduct, attitude, or behavior to make working there more professionally rewarding.

Are you thriving or just surviving? If thriving, are you noting your contributions and achievements?

If you are just surviving, are you adjusting to your current situation (in your conduct, attitude, and behavior) until you can properly plot your exit strategy?

Chapter Eight

Obtaining Feedback

*Negative feedback is better that none. I would
rather have a man hate me than overlook me. As
long as he hates me I make a difference.*

—Hugh Prather

How's Your Track Record?

Notice before, during, and after any sporting event the commentators are always noting a particular team or athlete's track record. They carefully examine and discuss at great length the number of games, races or competitions won or lost and all other metrics that speak to how well they compare to others. Ask any athlete on the other side of this routine evaluation and they will acknowledge it is brutal at times to hear how others view your performance. The more successful athletes use the information to fuel their own performance improvement.

Obtaining feedback is important to everyone's development. Even the most successful athletes, performers, and business leaders seek feedback to improve their performance. Once the lights are off, the music has stopped, the crowds are gone, and the cameras have stopped rolling, even the best performers are left with the lingering thought: "How did I really do?"

Learning from your mistakes and making the appropriate course correction when needed is probably one of the best ways to make progress in your career. However, most us admittedly need help in identifying when our career might be derailed by our performance, conduct, attitude, and behavior.

As an HR professional, you must take the time to sit in the spotlight and allow—no, *encourage*—the commentators to assess your track record. This is something we hate with a passion, for we typically already have a "sense" of where we know we need to grow and develop. We just don't want it said out loud. This vulnerability can make or break a person.

The problems we face cannot be solved with the thinking that created them.

—Albert Einstein

In fact, it could be criticism of you in your past that stopped you cold in your tracks before. After all, what can I do with comments like, "You are too short," "You look too young to pull off this job," or even "You're not ready." These are all comments given to me in past feedback. I couldn't grow taller, and stilettos weren't in fashion at the time. I couldn't suddenly age myself to appease an employer, and I certainly couldn't do anything about not being ready if my assessor wasn't specific.

Let's acknowledge that not everyone is good at offering feedback, and some feedback in our past has to be thrown out with the trash. But there is valuable feedback out there that you can use. There are aspects of your track record that have been career derailers and detractors that, upon reflection, you can use for growth and development. But where do you go for that kind of information? First you have to get in the mindset to obtain the feedback. Realize and acknowledge that no one is perfect, even your rater, so let go of ego, acknowledge what you already know about yourself, and be willing to learn a little more. For feedback to be effective—you know, something you are willing to use to improve—you go to people you trust to tell you the truth, unfiltered and unapologetic. Here's the catch: you still have a choice—you can take it or leave it. If you leave it, it has no power, and you likely will not benefit from its insights at all. If you take it—feedback—it has the power to make you better.

This section is about assessing *you,* not the HR department. As a professional in human resources, you must know how the department is viewed and is performing against standards and stated goals. The importance of the work performed by HR and the sheer volume of intake and outputs, let alone the nature of the work itself, requires that leading HR professionals seeking to build a world-class HR department assess HR's performance. If this is not something you are doing within your organization, how can you know how to improve the image and relevance of HR?

But right now, let's focus on *your* personal and professional development.

Feedback—Personal and Professional

Step 1

1. Indentify 5–7 people you trust to provide you with honest personal and professional feedback. Include at least one person from each of the following categories when possible: co-worker, supervisor, direct

report, family members, and friends. The more feedback you get, the easier it will be to see consistency in how you are perceived.

2. Tell your raters you are seeking personal and professional development and that you consider them someone you trust to give you honest, clear, and direct feedback. Tell them that not only would you like written feedback, but that you would like about 30 minutes to debrief with them in person or over the phone. Assure them it will be a listening session—you listening to them and asking questions for clarification. Ask them if they will be one of your raters. If they agree, go to item 3.

3. Go online to my website, www.pamelajgreen.com, and download the feedback instrument and instruction sheet found under the "Resources" tab.

4. Print and give it to each person, or e-mail it to them.

5. The instructions ask them to provide you with written feedback and return within 3 days—make note of this and send a reminder to them within 48 hours if you have not received a response.

   Neither all, nor even most, feedback you receive will likely be negative. There will be moments in reading the feedback and hearing the conversation that you'll say "ouch" to yourself, but let it remain just an "ouch." Taking it too personally will cause you to lose focus. Take anything you felt was negative and make it constructive. It is only constructive if you can use it to make you better.

Note: Once you receive the written feedback, schedule at least 15–30 minutes to review their comments. This is not an interrogation. If you can't handle some negative feedback, you are not ready to move forward. There is a very poignant bible verse that reads "A fool despises correction." You need to be able to ask questions about the feedback so you can create a clear picture of your strengths and improvement areas. If you have a reputation for not being able to receive even negative feedback, you may not receive any, or at best you'll receive very few responses. Likewise, you want to select people who will be honest. This is not a critique of their ability to assess you; it is merely their impression of you. You need people willing to present a balanced view. There is something good about everyone, so it shouldn't be all bad. Receiving this feedback shouldn't take more than one week if all those you've asked are cooperative.

6. As you receive feedback from each rater, complete the 360 feedback form below.

Step 2

Use the section below to summarize the feedback from all responses.

Character refers to your observable conduct, attitude, and behavior.

Topic	Refer #1 (Co-worker)	Refer #2 (Co-worker)
Character Strengths		
Character Vulnerabilities		
Comments		

Career refers to those skills and abilities needed to perform at a competent level in an organization.

Topic	Refer #1 (Friend)	Refer #2 (Friend)
Career Strengths		
Career Vulnerabilities		
Comments		

Refer #3 (Boss)	Refer #4 (Former Boss)	Refer #5 (Direct Report)	Refer #6 (Direct Report)

Refer #3 (Family Member)	Refer #4 (Family Member)

Step 3

Once you've received the feedback and held your discussions, send personal notes thanking them for their feedback. Summarize what you heard them say and offer assurance that you will use it to improve.

The individuals you've obtained this feedback from will be quietly observing you. They will watch to see if you are using the feedback to improve. Did you actually listen to what they said in the debrief? Were you really serious or was it just an act? They may ask you how you're doing on this journey. Your "performance" from this point forward will be more of an influencer than you can imagine. When you change, everything around you has to change to adjust to you, making positive improvements.

Step 4

- Before going to your mentor or coach, you'll need to begin pulling everything together. Answer these questions and summarize your thoughts below:

- When it comes to my character (conduct, attitude, and behavior), my strengths are:

- When it comes to my character (conduct, attitude, and behavior), my vulnerabilities are:

- As it relates to my performance, I'm very good at:

- In my personal life, my strengths are:

- As it relates to my performance, I need to work on:

- In my personal life, I need to work on:

- I like my (or believe I would like a) career track in HR because:

- Things I dislike or that concern me about an HR career:

- I'm most satisfied with the following things in my personal life right now:

- I'm most dissatisfied with the following things in my personal life right now:

- Based on the feedback, people find me...

Step 5

Share your feedback with your mentor and your coach. They will help you make sense of it from a career-planning perspective and help you sort through the feedback for the more salient pieces of information for your development.

Chapter Review

What are your reflections about this exercise?

Did you learn anything new about yourself?

How can you best leverage the feedback you've received?

CHAPTER NINE

Brand U

*If you don't brand yourself, other people will.
And I can guarantee you that they won't brand
you in the way that you want to be branded.*

—Catherine Kaputa

Creating Your Personal Brand

Imagine you open your front door one day and there are two boxes. Both boxes are exactly the same size and contain the exact same contents, only one box is so nicely gift wrapped that you hardly want to open it. The other box is a visibly damaged cardboard box, and clearly the contents are more than likely damaged. Which box do you choose?

Many employers are faced with this same dilemma every day. Two equally qualified candidates; however, one has a more polished personal brand than the other, a personal brand that would be a positive reflection of the organization itself. Yes, you in the nicely gift wrapped box, whose contents are neatly packaged to withstand the blows encountered during shipping, your box is the box that is most highly coveted. *This* is an example of your personal brand.

Your personal brand is how you want people to view you and the impression you want to leave with them. It is the perfect accoutrement to your bio, résumé, or portfolio. Do you want friends, family, constituents, or even strangers to see you as outgoing and friendly? Maybe resourceful, entrepreneurial, and intelligent are words you want to come to the minds of those you meet. Take a few moments and think about it. Using the results of the 360-degree feedback information you collected earlier in this process, what impression do you believe you are leaving behind? From what observable behaviors are you drawing this conclusion?

Think about this the next time you walk into a room: Based on how you are greeted—or not—what impression are you leaving? Go back to your survey results. How did your friends and family and co-workers respond to that question? How did your immediate supervisor respond?

None of us is perfect. This book isn't about perfection, but improvement. Every one of us has a place for improvement in our personal brand. Some will need major adjustments, others just minor tweaks. Regardless, you need to think about a plan for how will you make improvements. What behaviors can you exhibit that will leave a positive and lasting impression with almost everyone you encounter? Will it be your smile, your greeting, how well you listen to others, or the thoughtful questions you ask? Or will a negative attitude, poor personal and professional appearance, or lack of hygiene turn people off? All these things leave an impression on people, good and bad, whether we like it or not. Your personal image is part of your brand.

John Deere's slogan is "Nothing Runs Like a Deere." The business is built on the guarantee that its equipment will perform consistently. Farmers and contractors purchase this equipment because John Deere's reputation stands on its guarantee. If John Deere stopped delivering on its brand promise, consumers would be unhappy and find another brand. And because there are so many more competitors to John Deere today than yesterday, consumers don't have to worry if a comparable product will be available, because they *know* there will be. Likewise, if our personal brand is tarnished, our relationships will suffer. Employers, consumers of talent, will seek different employees to work on projects or fill assignments; our friends and family will reduce their interaction with us; and the list goes on.

Use the results of your 360-degree feedback in chapter 8 to create a brand development plan and identify what you will do to ensure you present a positive image and reputation. Ideas include:

- Return calls within 24 hours.
- Write thank-you notes or send an e-mail to those you've collected business cards from or otherwise encountered and want to remain in contact with.
- Be nicer to people.
- Develop better co-worker relationships.
- Ensure your appearance is professional at all times, dressing appropriately for each occasion, including the job and work environment.
- Maintain a polished physical presence.
- Maintain eye contact and offer a firm handshake (yes, this is *still* important) when greeting people.
- Have an exceptional customer service attitude.
- Improve your listening skills.
- Refrain from being curt with people.

In the next section, take some time to again review the feedback you received and complete your brand development plan.

Brand Development Plan

The steps I will take to improve personally based on the feedback and my own self-assessment are:

What	When	Where
Handling my emotions	Immediately	Contact my company's Employee Assistance Program to help identify next steps.
Work on improving my personal appearance by dressing more appropriately for the work environment	Over 90 days	Explore consignment shops in the area and layaway options at my local retailer and put more effort into ensuring my clothing fits properly and that I have a professional appearance.

Who Will Help (me overcome obstacles)	How Will This Help My Career
Read a self-help book in the next 30 days and work to respond appropriately to other people regardless of the situation.	Mastering this will help me be received better by co-workers, family, and friends. It will help me build relationships so that I can move forward toward my future.
Ask a friend who has great personal style to assist me. I will also seek the help of a personal shopper at my local retailer.	It will improve my self-esteem and help me feel more confident in the work environment. I don't want my appearance to significantly hinder any potential career development or promotional opportunities.

Your Brand Promise

Every brand has a brand promise associated with it, and the HR profession, because it is a service within the organization, is a type of brand. Because you are an HR professional, your identity is tied to your brand. Now, think about how HR is branded within your organization. Are you responsible for how the HR brand is viewed in your organization? Have you contributed in anyway positively or negatively to the image of the brand? By examining the implicit and explicit promises HR makes in the organization, you can literally turn around the image of the HR brand. Likewise, as an HR professional, you must begin to examine the implicit and explicit promises you make within your function in the organization.

Your brand promise is less of a statement and more of an attitude of excellence. It is what people expect from you based mostly on what you do and how they interact with you. You can write an HR mission or vision and hang it on a gold plaque, but if it isn't communicated in your behavior, you will not be viewed as believable, credible, or trustworthy. Believe it or not, everyone has a brand promise, more implicit than explicit. What do people expect from you? What can they consistently expect to receive from their relationship or interaction with you? Let me give you an example.

I have a business manager whom I can rely on to maintain confidences, pay attention to detail, efficiently manage the budget, monitor all expenses, and meet deadlines. She's responsive and responsible, and few things, if any, fall through the cracks. If I were to write her brand promise, it would be: Joan Jet (not her real name) "a loyal team player and superstar performer who plays her position well and consistently delivers on results. If she were a basketball player, she would be Michael Jordan!"

Not delivering on your promise will result in a damaged brand image. Everyone around you expects something from you. It is up to you to set the tone for their level of expectation. All disappointment comes from unmet expectations. Set the bar at a height that stretches you, even a little, to improve your brand, but not so much that you will constantly disappoint yourself and others. If you are currently not a timely person, then you are delivering on a brand promise that you will almost always be late. What does this say to your employer, family, or friends? Who is counting on you to be more timely? Can you adjust your behavior to improve your brand promise to be timely in everything you do? I think so. Think about it this way: if you needed to create a tagline to put under your signature every time you signed your name, every time your name was printed, or even on your business cards, what would it be?

Now in the space below, jot down some adjectives and ideas that you can use to help brand your image:

Extending and Showcasing Your Brand

There are a number of ways to showcase and leverage your personal brand. If you were a product, you'd want someone to take notice and pull you off the shelf. As a professional, you want your colleagues and business leaders to take notice and pull you into the business.

In the old days we showcased our brand through our performance, establishing goals and meeting or beating deadlines and delivering results. We extended a firm handshake, maintained eye contact, and had a strong personal appearance. We didn't stop there, but when needed we could present a professionally written résumé, a solid personal and professional reference, and the good ol' printed calling cards. And guess what? All of these things are still very important. But thanks to the increased use and reliance upon the Internet, social technology, reality television, casual dress codes, tattoos, piercings, the increased ability to work from home or anywhere in the world, the influences of global culture and popular media, texting, tweeting, You-Tubing, Skypeing, virtual magazines, and virtual everything, showcasing your brand just got a whole lot easier—or has it?

> *An image is not simply a trademark, a design, a slogan or an easily remembered picture. It is a studiously crafted personality profile of an individual.*
>
> —Daniel J. Boorstin

Blogging has brought out the closet journalist in all of us, hasn't it? There are some top-notch professional and personal blogs in social media, and then there are some downright ugly and unprofessional blogs dominating the Internet as well. My concern isn't as much for those being attacked in blogs as much as it is for the writers. If you are an HR professional and have something to say, just keep in mind that once it's out there, it's out there *forever*!

Have you snagged your name as a domain name yet? When was the last time you did a Google search for your name? Stop and try it now. What did you find? Were you pleased with what was written? We need to conduct periodic searches of our names in social media to monitor our virtual image. If you want to "get your name out there," you've got to get involved and decide what you want your voice to be. This is tougher than it sounds. So start slow, observe others who are expressing themselves virtually, and take a planned and thoughtful approach. Part of branding yourself is also protecting your name and controlling the image of your brand—what is being said, written, and communicated about you, to the extent possible of course. Snagging your domain name is an important and effective way of influencing how you are viewed. By registering your name as a URL, and subsequently creating a professional website, you can have a significantly positive impact on you and your organization.

Finally, keep an eye on what is being said about your organization on sites like Vault.com and the Glassdoor.com. HR can take a pretty tough beating virtually, but as an influencer of the HR brand image, especially for your organization, you can affect how your organization is viewed in social technology.

Your Professional Portfolio

A career or professional portfolio is a collection of your best work over the years. More and more professionals are looking for a way to stand out and showcase their personal and professional brand. Before the onslaught of personal websites to showcase your brand, career or professional portfolios were initially contained in file folders; then they progressed to nicely designed ring binders, followed by colorful and impressive PowerPoint presentations, and finally web presence, which is often very creative, innovative, and professional looking. With the creation of the iPad and similar portable computing devices, you can leave that huge ring binder at home, upload your PowerPoint to your iPad, and share it during an interview. Regardless of the format, your portfolio is a collection of your employment experiences, significant accomplishments, and proof of your skills and capabilities. It should provide tangible examples of work you have performed and recognition received as a result of your achievements over the years.

A sample electronic portfolio can be found by visiting my website at **www.pamelajgreen.com**. Not quite at the techno-geek level that I'm trying to achieve? A written portfolio, like the ones outlined below, are just as easy to create. The hardest part is collecting all the data. Lets first review the elements of a student portfolio and then a career portfolio.

Student Portfolio

A student portfolio should be created by high school or college students with limited or no work experience, who want to showcase academic and scholastic achievements. This 3–5-page PowerPoint presentation should outline the following:

Cover Page

Your name, address, phone number, and e-mail address

Pages 2–3

Personal and career aspirations

Short-term career goals

Long-term career goals

Academic achievements

Volunteer achievements

2-3 endorsements/quotes

Other accomplishments

Page 4

Thank you!

Repeat contact information

Career Portfolio

A career portfolio is for anyone who can demonstrate and thus wants to showcase career achievements. This, again, is best conveyed as a PowerPoint presentation, largely because of the sheer volume of résumés potential employers receive on a daily basis. Follow their normal online submission process, and when you secure the interview, take printed color copies with you to the interview, unless the company has gone "green," in which case printed color copies could offend them. If this is the case, send the electronic portfolio to them in advance and take it on your iPad. This way you can be prepared to conduct a mini presentation on your iPad if printing is not an option.

A basic career portfolio outline would cover:

Cover Page

> Your name, address, phone number, and e-mail address

Page 1

> Your mission/vision statement
>
> Brief introduction

Page 2

> Your vitae
>
> Some people like to include their picture; others do not—the choice is yours

Page 3

> Chronological work experience

Page 4

> Strategic accomplishments

Page 5

> Certificates, certifications, degrees, honors, etc.
>
> Professional associations/memberships
>
> Volunteer experience

Page 5

> Thank you!
>
> Repeat contact information

Getting Started

Step 1: Start by collecting and organizing everything you can find that supports your academic and career achievements. Every piece of paper, pictures, trophies, awards, letters, acknowledgements, articles, news clippings, note cards, performance reviews, letters of recommendation, diplomas, certifications, certificates, and so forth.

Step 2: Then write down every professional achievement you can recall and show proof of—at the end you'll need to go back and organize in chronological order. For example, if you've lead project teams, designed programs, created and executed strategic initiatives, reduced turnover, improved employee satisfaction and engagement, improved staff retention , increased revenue, designed programs and plans, and so on, you'll want to make note of those things, including the dates, times, outcomes, and so forth.

Step 3: Make a list of your volunteer achievements, including years, positions held, and contributions made.

Step 4: Organize as outlined above.

Step 5: Select a PowerPoint presentation template that is professional looking. Stay away from plain white presentations. If you do this, why waste your time in PowerPoint? Just stick with the résumé. You'll want to showcase some creativity, but you're in HR—how would you present a portfolio to you? Also review the examples found on **www.pamelajgreen.com** and keep in mind font size and readability.

Step 6: If applying for a job, follow the company's protocol for application. Send a separate cover letter and traditional résumé, and reference how they can view your career portfolio inside your cover letter and on your resume.

Your Online Presence

I am an admirer of technology. While I do have a Facebook page and LinkedIn and Twitter accounts, the time to manage these systems can be tough to find daily. However, social technology continues to improve, and increasingly the interaction between technologies is getting easier and more efficient. Let's take a look at a few more popular social technology activities:

Blogging
Wikipedia defines a blog as a blend of the term *web log,* which is usually part of a website, though many blogs are websites in and of themselves. Maintained mostly by individuals who have commentary, news, or information they wish to share with an audience, blogging either corporately or individually has many benefits. It allows you hone and sharpen your writing and communication skills. It can be an effective way for you to showcase your brand and your strengths, and finally, if you are selling a product or service, it can increase web traffic and lead to increased sales. An interactive blog allows you to expand your network and can create job leads and help you fill open positions for your employer.

Blogging is not for everyone. It requires regular updates, diligence, and some creativity, especially as more and more people get into blogging—you'll want to differentiate yourself. A word of caution to those current and would-be bloggers: be mindful of what you say and the tone you express. Be intentional in how you communicate. You must decide how you want to convey your image to your audience, not just for the short run, but for the long run.

Social Media and Tweeting

Many professionals limit their Facebook interaction to family and personal friends. They find it a place to reconnect with old friends and to let their hair down—a little. As for LinkedIn—well, it is one of the most popular business Rolodexes online! It is a terrific way to connect with people you've just met and to maintain professional acquaintances with countless numbers of people. As you meet people in person, remember to go online and connect with them when you get back to the office. It is a wonderful tool. Twitter defines it's social presence as "a social networking and micro-blogging service that allows you answer the question, *'What are you doing?'* by sending short text messages 140 characters in length, called 'tweets,' to your friends, or 'followers.'" Every HR professional needs to check it out and play around. You'd be surprised who's "out there."

Regardless of your future plans, keep them in mind as you engage in the virtual world of social networking. Establish a solid professional presence and manage your time effectively. Also, be mindful of company policy about engaging in social technology.

Leveraging Your Networks

With over 700 contacts in LinkedIn at the time of this writing, I find it difficult to reach out to those in this network as well as other contacts I have established on a regular and routine basis. In an effort to stay connected, send periodic updates about what you are doing to stay in touch. If you hear of job opportunities, blast a note to those in your contact list. Acknowledge major events such as voting to get people to get out the vote. Announce special events occurring in your life. Have you been written up in a local paper or received online press or special recognition? Announce your new book or other event about to take place to the entire group. And a good ol' standby is to acknowledge the holiday season and send a note to everyone seeking to stay in touch in the New Year. Don't forget to update your picture and profile often. All these things keep people interested in what you are doing, and this interest could serve you well when you decide to launch a new business or other venture that could general additional income for you and your family.

Other ways to leverage your network is to pick someone to have lunch with or call at least once a week. Spending 20–30 minutes a week is not bad to make sure you stay top of mind. Send a card, remember a birthday or anniversary, do something to stay connected. To leverage means to influence. Which of your contacts in your network are you influencing? How are you benefiting from having established such a great network of people? How are your contacts benefiting from knowing you? How often do you ask those who've poured into your life, "What I can do for you?"

Meet-ups!

The word is newer than the activity itself and describes meeting in person with people, many of whom you might have met virtually. When meeting with Twitter friends and followers, you're said to have a "tweet-up." Meet-ups are not limited to virtual friends connecting in person—they are also for local friends, acquaintances, business contacts, and yes, other HR professionals and contacts just wanting to find time to connect socially. Meet-ups are happy hours on fire! There is very little to organize, especially since there is no agenda, no money to handle, and no registrations to coordinate. It can be as simple as sending out an e-mail and inviting people to connect or more complex. Visit **www.meetup.com** for details on how you can organize your own HR meet-up.

Chapter Review

Compare your initial thoughts about branding yourself to your thoughts right now. Are you more or less interested in working on your personal and professional brand?

What obstacles might you encounter in your work environment when you embark on improving your brand, and how might you address those challenges?

Review your company's ethics, code of conduct, and intellectual property policies and procedures. Make note of any concerns you have below and discuss them with appropriate parties.

Assess whether a career portfolio is for you. How might you leverage that type of communication?

Of the various types of branding methods described above, what most resonates with you?

CHAPTER TEN

The Plan

*It is a terrible thing to see and
have no vision.*

—Helen Keller

Where Am I Going and
How Will I Get There?

By now you should feel you have a clearer sense of direction, including who you are and how you are viewed by your co-workers, family, and friends. You should also have an unambiguous picture of your strengths and improvement areas, as well as a plan for making necessary adjustments.

So, what do you want to do with this information? Let's begin with the end. Remember the work you completed in chapter 3, the End Game Summary? Using that information and the feedback you received in the chapter 8 exercises, and the reflective exercises you've completed, use this section and the remainder of this book to identify the HR career track you should be on and get onto that path.

Figuring out the path you want to take is just one aspect of managing your HR career. How will your HR career path meet up with your retirement plans? This will sound strange, I know, but in reality, very few of us HR professionals take our own advice. Waiting to manage your career until you have children and tons of financial responsibilities might seem a bit late, but there is still time. Starting today, even if you were not trained about money management and even still struggle with it, it is not too late.

Having a financial management strategy for yourself personally and professionally can help you understand how your organization manages its finances. It takes financial resources to manage your career and to ensure that you have options to make moves when the right opportunities present themselves. If you control and manage your money properly, you also control your future. If you cannot control your money, you become a slave to your job, and well, all the work you're putting in

---
Clarity affords focus.

—Thomas Leonard

---

here means nothing. Money is a resource that provides you with options. Putting financial resources away (yes, I'm talking about savings) means that should opportunities come, issues arise, or tragedy occur, you can rest assured knowing that your options have been multiplied because you have resources to finance your decision.

When a person makes a personal investment in something, they are more likely to care for it and make wise decisions concerning that investment to yield a greater return. There is a difference in how my young son cares for things my husband and I purchase for him than in how he cares for the things he purchases with his own money. The difference is absolutely amazing. Because of his attitude toward money and how we are raising him to handle finances, we wonder if we shouldn't allow him to be responsible for handling our finances!

The point here is your career is your investment. This means that you believe so much in yourself and your future that you are willing to invest the time and resources needed to advance and develop professionally.

Don't allow what you see around you or your current circumstance prevent you from moving into your career path. Yes, external realities should inform and provide insight for planning and timing, but they shouldn't deter or distract you—you simply have to plan around the present or impending situation.

Some things to do immediately:

- Stop spending excess money and living outside your means.
- Read a book on money management. There are some really good authors, including:

  Robert Kiyosaki, *Rich Dad* series

  Dave Ramsey, *Total Money Makeover*

  Michelle Singletary, The Color of Money column for the *Washington Post*
- Seek free advice and talk to people who handle their money well.
- Set up a bill payment and money management schedule
- If your situation is critical, contact your local consumer credit counseling agency for immediate assistance and relief. They can contact your creditors and set up reasonable payments.
- Start saving something, even if it is $10 a week or a paycheck. Get in the habit of putting money aside.

HR Career Analysis

Now that we've addressed the importance of managing your personal finances and how it can affect the decisions you make about your career, let's focus our attention on fine-tuning your career goals. Every job assignment has a requisite set of skills and competencies to accomplish the task efficiently and effectively. It is not just about landing your dream HR job; you want to ensure you are prepared to take on the assignment and be proficient in it. In addition, every organization has a culture and another set of expectations that you'll have to adjust to. Therefore, moving forward in HR depends on how well you assess the difference between where you are now and where you would like to go:

- Will you need additional education or experience?
- Are there certificates, certification, or licensure you are required to obtain and maintain?
- How many hours in a day/week will you be expected to perform?
- Is there travel associated with this career? Is travel something you are looking for?
- What is the income potential for where you live (or in other parts of the country) in this career?
- What is the availability of work for this career in this geographic area?
- Are you limited right now to a specific geographic area or are you free to relocate?
- What are the health and safety risks associated with work in HR in this company or geographic area?

Knowing the answers to these questions and evaluating other statistics about human resources can help you chart a more accurate career path. Comprehensive sources of HR-related information and statistics can be found at:

- The U.S. Bureau of Labor Statistics (BLS) (www.bls.gov)
- The National Compensation Survey (www.bls.gov/ncs)
- BLS Occupational Employment Statistics (www.bls.gov/oes)
- The U.S. Department of Labor (www.dol.gov)
- The U.S. Equal Employment Opportunity Commission (www.eeoc.gov)

The Society for Human Resource Management and your state and local web pages will have tons of valuable information regarding local occupational outlook and career statistics as well as employment outlook data. Do your homework.

Frequently Asked Questions

Let's explore some of the most frequently asked human resource-related career questions:

Should I obtain certification?

Yes. Obtaining HR credentials speaks to the HR professional's practical knowledge of the field of HR and capability in practical application and work experience. Even if you are in a senior human resource position, consider certification because it demonstrates to junior staff a commitment to the profession and ensures that you too stay abreast of changes in the profession.

Which HR certification should I go for?

Obtain an HR certification in an area of HR that best aligns with your HR focus area. Keep in mind that the combination of certification with education and experience makes for a stronger candidate. Here are just a few to consider:

- Certified Benefits Professional (CBP), administered by World at Work

- Certified Compensation Professional (CCP), administered by World at Work

- Certified Employee Benefits Specialist (CEBS) administered by International Foundation of Employee Benefits Plans

- Certified Professional in Learning and Performance Certification (CPLP), administered by the American Society for Training and Development

- Compensation Management Specialist (CMS) administered by International Foundation of Employee Benefits Plans

- Global Professional in Human Resources (GPHR) administered by the HR Certification Institute

- Professional in Human Resources (PHR) administered by the HR Certification Institute

- Senior Professional in Human Resources (SPHR) administered by the HR Certification Institute

What is the occupational outlook for HR in the U.S. and globally?

The U.S. Bureau of Labor Statistics projects that the HR profession will grow at a rate that is 10% faster than all other occupations by 2018. This rapid growth and demand for HR excellence will require present and future HR professionals to continually assess and develop their HR competency to ensure they achieve and maintain a competitive advantage.

Should I take the PHR and then the SPHR when I'm eligible, or should I just wait and take the SPHR?

Take the PHR when you're eligible. Don't wait. Certification is about demonstrating competence and forces you to stay on top of the profession. You want to demonstrate competence now, not years from now. If you feel you need to take the SPHR, you should, but you don't have to. You're just as credible as a PHR regardless of your level now and into the future.

Should I specialize or generalize?

Depends on what your self-assessment and feedback was in this process. What do you like to do? Where do you tend to spend your time? Which area of HR is most attractive to you? It is easier to move from generalist to specialist if you are able to demonstrate competence and deliverables in a specialist area. Moving from specialist to generalist is tougher if you try to do so when moving from one position to another type of position outside the company because outsiders don't know what your daily work has been. If you've held the title manager of employee relations for 3 years, then moving to manager of compensation and benefits or HR manager could prove difficult outside the organization. Internally, however, it becomes much easier. Try to make the transition where you are first building your skills in that new area of HR.

How do I go about understanding the financials?

Ask someone. Start with someone at work who is in a manager or director role who wouldn't mind mentoring you in this area. Talk directly with a finance person at work. Humble yourself and just admit what you don't know and start from there. Engaging someone at work will make what you learn real. It will literally come to life, and the lesson continues every month when financials are completed. If you don't feel comfortable with someone at work, then talk to someone outside work who can offer assistance. Check your network for local referrals. Another thing to do is take a class and get a tutor. The key is repetition and getting focused.

MBA or MLHR?

If your undergraduate degree is in human resources, then perhaps an option for you would be to focus your master's level degree on business to round out your education nicely. If your undergraduate degree was in a non-HR area then perhaps your master's degree should be in human resources. If, however, your undergraduate degree was in business, then the obvious move for you would be the master's degree in HR.

What are the best ways to develop skills or competencies?

Developing a new skill or improving one requires exposure and practice. Who is doing it well and what you can learn from them? What books or resources can you read to give you insight? How can you get some practice? Look for opportunities to first learn how skilled individuals perform and learn from them. Then get your practice time in. Volunteering is one way, but seeking the opportunity to develop something new on the job is another. Obtaining a mentor or coach to help provide you with insight is also helpful.

For-profit or not-for-profit?

Having worked in not-for-profit and for-profit organizations, I can tell you there are fewer differences today than yesterday. It all depends on the entity. You must do your homework. Not-for-profits will pay for critical talent and key performers just as well as for-profit entities. Size matters as well. In larger organizations you're likely to have more layers and a wider range of HR opportunities available. In smaller organizations, you might find you're wearing all HR hats with little to no room for specialization. Moving from not-for-profit to for-profit and vice versa also depend on how you communicate your skills and capabilities. What have you done? What are you doing? and How did your company benefit? are all questions you should be prepared to convey to potential employers when seeking career changes in HR. Staying too long in a not-for-profit could make moving to HR in a for-profit entity difficult if you don't have a track record for having worked in a for-profit organization. However, not-for-profits, though weary of salary expectations, often open their welcoming arms to for-profit professionals. Culture shock is a dirty word that no one can prepare you for in any transition, and even if they did, would you believe them? Just remember: no company is perfect!

Does volunteer experience really count?

Volunteering can be a great way to gain valuable work experience, meet new people, build your professional network, gain experience in a new career field, and find your next career opportunity. It is also a way to give back to your community and to support a charitable organization. Don't discount the tremendous value volunteering can bring and the skills you can build as a result of a few extra hours a week or month. Volunteering counts if you demonstrate how you benefited from it.

Many employers seek individuals who have a well-balanced sense of themselves and their communities. The fact that you have a passion, interests, or desires outside your professional life demonstrates strength of character and commitment to balancing work, family, and personal time. If you are not or have never had this experience, it's worth exploring.

HR Career Plan Summary

Let's pull it all together:

Based on the feedback I've received, the assessments I've taken, and my own reflections and research, I believe I will pursue the following HR discipline or HR focus:	
I want to work at the following level in HR over the next 3–5 years (manager, director, executive, etc.):	
My motivation for pursuing a career in HR is:	
What things in my personal life, if any, are potential obstacles? (e.g., finances, family commitment, childcare, etc.)	

How can I overcome these obstacles?	
What professional skills or competencies will I need to work to develop?	
Who is missing from my board of directors?	
What type of company might I be best suited to work in, if not my current company?	

What behaviors can help me get more satisfaction out of my HR career?	
What is my exit strategy? How will I navigate my career if a company cannot live up to my expectations?	

Skill Gap Analysis

Recognize that there are often many steps to achieving your ultimate career goal. Some professionals may be only months away from achieving their career plans in HR; for others, it may take a little longer, so let's focus on achievements in feasible increments. Use the skill gap analysis form below to identify the skills, abilities, and experiences you'll realistically need to get in the game and thrive as an HR professional and business leader.

HR Career Goal: *Director of HR for a small business*

	Existing Skill Set	Skills Required*	Skills I Need to Develop
Education	Undergraduate Degree in Human Resource Management	Master's Degree in Business	Need to complete degree before pursuing new career opportunity.

HR Career Goal:

	Existing Skill Set	Skills Required	Skills I Need to Develop
Education			
Certifications, Certificates or Licensure			
Related Training			
Skills			
Competencies			
Other			

(*) Here you want to identify the basic requirements for your transition – for an employer to consider you as a viable candidate.

Human Resources Career Management Cycle
Step 1: Get Focused
Step 2: Assess Business Acumen
Step 3: Get Needed Training and Development
Step 4: Seek Counsel and Support
Step 5: Obtain Feedback
Step 6: Implement

Step 1: Get Focused

Explore the field of human resources. What is this profession? What are the possible career paths? How is success defined? What are the challenges facing the profession, and are you up to meeting those challenges? Chapters 1 can help with this, but it could require additional work on your part, like talking to professionals in the field. This step is also helpful for those wishing to change HR focus or wanting to go to the next level in their HR career.

Is HR the career for you? How can what you like to do complement work in HR and vice versa? If not a new career, this step is for those interested in changing the type of work they are performing in the HR field. You might be changing from compensation to benefits or generalist to employee relations specialist, for example. These types of moves should be evaluated carefully to ensure that area of specialty is the best fit for you.

Here is also where you begin to make some decisions about the type of work you want to achieve in the profession. Look at your life cycle and make some decisions on what retirement looks like and how a career in HR can help you achieve your personal goals. Annually assess and reassess where you are and if you've gotten off track from your career plans. Here is where you make a U-turn if needed or are reassured that you are headed in the right direction.

Step 2: Assess Business Acumen

The business world changes every minute of the day. Are you keeping up with the requirements of the new demands that face your business? This knowledge will help you stay relevant and build your credibility as a business leader and an HR professional.

Step 3: Get Needed Training and Development

Explore and define the type of training and development you need to achieve your career goals. Will training courses meet your development needs, or will you need to pursue a degree program?

Step 4: Seek Counsel and Support

Who have you included in your circle of advisors? Do you have a mentor or coach? Who is providing you with guidance through your career and work-related decisions? Securing wise counsel will help you as you move throughout your career.

Step 5: Obtain Feedback

We all need feedback. It helps us know if we are headed in the right direction, assimilating without losing our brand identity, and where exactly we need to correct our course. It is also the way in which we build relationships and obtain positive information about things we're doing well. Obtain feedback on the completion of every major project or career turn. Don't wait until an annual review—lots of information gets lost in that timeframe.

Step 6: Implement

What plans or ideas are you holding onto that you need to release? What classes do you need to take? What applications need to be completed? What books or articles need to be written? What certifications are you waiting to secure? Get these things on your timetable and launch them.

Repeat steps 5 through 6 within 30 days following your annual performance review. If none, then schedule a time annually to assess your progress against your timeline.

Working Your Plan

Below is an outline of the types of activities that can go into your career management plan. These will of course be determined by your personal development needs and the direction you wish to take your HR career and organizational obligations.

Plan	1st Quarter	2nd Quarter	3rd Quarter	4th Quarter
Corporate Strategic Plan	Explore BRIC* growth.	Narrow focus.	Write business plan.	Execute business plan.
Business Unit Plans	Determine the what, why, how of your career and identify barriers to entry and workarounds.	Research tax, legal & technology implications.	Determine exact source of revenue stream and payment options.	Test systems and ensure readiness to launch.
Human Resource Plan	Develop engagement and communication plan. Assess internal capabilities.	Research HR implications and what effect, if any, other trends will have on workforce.	Create / launch talent acquisition and management strategy.	Ensure talent is in place and employees are engaged and informed.
Career Plan	Refresh your training and development in global employment regulations and practices.	Do your homework— who else has done this?	Read literature and seek counsel from those who've had some experience in the area.	Build and engage your network for insight and feedback.
Specific Goals	Complete refresher course [name course] by [date].	Identify 3–4 companies by [date].	Connect with the HR leaders from companies identified previously. Research articles (magazine, online, or from nearest library).	Touch base (or seek to build your network) with those who might be similarly situated.

*BRIC: Brazil, Russia, India, and China

Achieving Career and Organizational Alignment

One of the best ways to ensure career growth is by determining where your company is headed and then identify opportunities to build your skills along with the growth of the company. For example, a model might look like the table on the previous page.

Here is how it aligns with the HR Career Management Cycle:

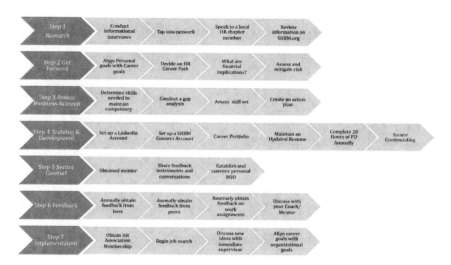

As you begin to align your career goals, at least in part, with your company's strategic direction, you can ensure that as the company grows you grow. This is an excellent model to help anyone reporting to you achieve career growth and success with the company.

Chapter Review

Do your personal finances align with your career goals? If not, are you taking the necessary actions to get aligned?

Review the exercises in this chapter. Does it help you to focus when your career goals are aligned with your company's?

What excites you about moving forward?

CHAPTER ELEVEN

Time Management

Time stays long enough for those who use it.

—Leonardo da Vinci

Your Schedule

You are responsible for you. If something is going to happen, you're the one who has to make it happen. Even an unemployed person has to first look for a job in order to obtain one, so get focused and move forward. Some of us need to rearrange our entire life to work toward our career goals. Others may need to make only some minor adjustments. Stop and reflect on what you want to do each week and then each day by asking yourself these questions:

Where do I need to spend my time?

Are there appointments I need to make and keep?

Are there people I need to speak with?

This means examining everything you are doing from the time you wake up in the morning to the time you go to bed at night! If you need to rearrange your daily routine, here are some tips for stretching those hours in the day and meeting goals:

Get up 30–45 minutes earlier each day.

Shower the night before to save time in the morning.

Carve out an "Hour of Power" on your calendar in addition to a solid lunch break.

Prepare lunch the night before to ensure you eat properly.

Drink plenty of water daily. Water is our body's only means of flushing out toxins, a major factor in disease prevention. Additionally, our energy level is significantly affected by the amount of water we drink. It has been medically proven that just a 5% drop in body fluids will cause a 25% to 30% loss of energy in the average person.

Get some reading time in during lunch or take a brisk walk for a mental and/or physical refresh.

See if your employer offers flexible work arrangements to permit you to take classes at the local college or university, or an online program.

Either you run the day or the day runs you.

—Jim Rohn

Seek the assistance of family members and friends to provide childcare backup when needed.

Remember the crock pot? Use it—saves tons of time, and you have a hot meal waiting for you when you get home, so you can get back an hour or two to focus on your development.

Prepare your meals for the week on the weekend. Freeze in appropriately sized containers and thaw/heat daily.

Significantly reduce the amount of time you spend in front of the television and on computers playing games.

Use your early morning extra time for exercise or get 30 minutes of exercise in at lunch or a few hours before bedtime.

In the space below, describe additional ways you can adjust your schedule to work toward and accomplish your career goals:

Time Management

Get Organized

Everyone knows someone they would honor with "The Most Unorganized Person in the World" award! These are people who might keep everything just in case they might need it later. They maintain little pieces of paper, lots of them, with names, addresses, phone numbers, and notes that they may or may not refer to as needed. Perhaps their file system is a stack, or rather several stacks of papers on their desk, floor, or in plastic tubs. While the list goes on, the test for true organization depends on the ease with which someone else could quickly and easily find needed information in your personal space (desk, home office, etc.) either in your absence or under your direction. We like to dismiss disorganized people by letting them off the hook with statements like, "Well, if that is *their* system and it works for *them* . . ." or "As long as they can find what they need. . . ." But this is impractical. At some point sooner or later, someone is going to need something in your absence. How easily will it be for them to find it? We owe it to others around us—family, friends, and co-workers—to get our lives organized.

Getting organized will save you time searching—period. It will also reduce the stress associated with disorder, and it will help increase your ability to become more productive. Below are some tips to help you get better organized:

- Purchase a personal computer system. Never use employer systems for personal use.
- Clean, organize and purge your desk or home office.
- No home office? Carve out a place for "you" time at home.

- Make a checklist. There are great electronic checklists for iPad users such as Omnifocus and ToodleDo.
- Use only one calendar for both personal and business needs.
- Use a computer calendar system and use the notification feature to ensure your computer sends reminders.
- Use Outlook or a similar system to list and keep track of your goals.
- Update you contacts/network lists. If there literally are 6 people between you and your next career opportunity, who are they? Are they in your contact list? How do you get to know them?

What are some other ways you can get organized?

_____

_____

_____

_____

_____

_____

_____

_____

_____

Book Summary

Recognize that HR today is less about solving problems and more about creating solutions; it is as much about saving money as it is about adding value.

Have an eye on the future talent pool: workforce planning/readiness, young professionals, emerging leaders.

Remain a student of Human Resources. As your company changes, so should you and your HR program.

Stay abreast of global, legal, governmental, local demographic, technological, and economic shifts and the impact on HR and your business. Sound the alarms when necessary but learn to forecast and help the company prepare for change.

I have only just a minute,
Only 60 seconds in it,
Forced upon me—can't refuse it,
Didn't seek it, didn't choose it,
But it's up to me to use it.
I must suffer if I lose it,
Give account, if I abuse it.
Just a tiny little minute –
But eternity is in it!

—Benjamin E. Mays

Find the determination to be a success in HR regardless of whether you're a graduating student, lifetime HR professional, just passing through, or had HR dumped on you. . . . Go ahead and succeed anyway.

Find the area of HR that works for you. You may have to try a few on for size, but when you find the HR shoe you like, and it fits, wear it well!

Be prepared for a good fight every now and then. You know you've got the ball and are headed toward the in zone when people are blocking you and trying to distract you and get you off focus. A strong personal and professional network, your coaches, and your mentors will help you stay focused on your stated goals.

Seek to create win-win outcomes and to be an innovator and influencer wherever you go and whenever possible.

Not just anyone can "do" HR; many will try, and few will succeed. You can ensure success by regularly obtaining and using objective feedback about your performance.

Give yourself a career makeover and adjust your style as the profession changes and as your company changes.

Conduct your gap analysis; improve your skillset as needed to tighten the gap and enjoy a successful career in HR.

Bibliography

"Blog." *Wikipedia, the Free Encyclopedia.* Web. Spring 2011, http://en.wikipedia.org/wiki/Blog.

Canton, James. "Top Ten Trends." *Institute for Global Futures,* www.globalfuturist.com/about-igf/top-ten-trends.html.

"Changes in the Workplace Reveal New Realities for Multigenerational Workforce." *World at Work.* 27 May 2008, www.worldatwork.org/waw/adimLink?id=26533.

"Create a Business Case." *Project Management Templates, Template Tools and Life Cycle,* www.Method123.com.

"Employment Trends in the 21st Century." *International Center for Peace & Development,* www.icpd.org/employment/Empltrends21century.htm.

Florida State University. Informational Interviews. Raw data. Florida State University.

Green, Pamela, and Society for Human Resource Management. "From Backpack to Briefcase." SHRM Regional Student Conference. Seattle, Washington. Winter 2010. Speech.

Groysberg, Boris, L. Kevin Kelly, and Bryan MacDonald. "The New Path to the C-Suite." *Harvard Business Review.* Mar. 2011: 60–68.

"Information Society." *Wikipedia, the Free Encyclopedia,* http://en.wikipedia.org/wiki/Information_society.

Karoly, Lynn A., and Constantijn W. A. Panis. *The 21st Century at Work: Forces Shaping the Future Workforce and Workplace in the United States.* Santa Monica, CA: RAND, 2004, www.rand.org/pubs/monographs/MG164.html.

"LMI Learning (NGRF)—Labour Market Changes."

NGRF—Welcome to the National Guidance Research Forum. LMI Learning (NGRF), www.guidance-research.org/lmi-learning/changing/changes.

Lombardo, Michael M., and Robert W. Eichinger. *The Career Architect Development Planner: An Expert System Offering 95 Research Based and Experience Tested Development Plans and Coaching Tips for Learners, Supervisors, Managers, Mentors, and Feedback Givers.* Minneapolis, MN: Lominger, 2000.

ManpowerGroup. "Entering The Human Age: A New Era." *ManpowerGroup.* 15 June 2011, www.manpowergroup.com/humanage/entering-the-human-age.html.

Mathis, Robert L., and John Harold Jackson. *Human Resource Management.* Cincinnati, OH: South-Western College Pub., 2000.

Maxwell, John C., and Jim Dornan. *Becoming a Person of Influence: How to Positively Impact the Lives of Others.* Nashville, TN: T. Nelson, 1997.

McEldowney, Gary. "Next Time You Want Something To Drink-Read On." *Allergy Consumer Review,* www.allergyconsumerreview.com/next-time-you-want-something-to-drink-read-on.html.

Mig, Cat. "10 Benefits Of Networking." Made Manual. *Mademan.com,* www.mademan.com/mm/10-benefits-networking.html.

Mooney, Kelly, and Laura Bergheim. "Introduction." *The Ten Demandments: Rules to Live by in the Age of the Demanding Consumer.* New York: McGraw-Hill, 2002, xiii—11.

Nguyen, Peter. "3 Types of Networking." *LinkedIn User Manual.* Talentelle.com, 5 Jan. 2007, http://linkedinusermanual.blogspot.com/2007/01/3-types-of-networking.html.

"Recruiting the Next Generation [Wandel Der Arbeitswelt]." *Recruiting the Next Generation,* www.recruitingthenextgeneration.de/index.php?article_id=34.

Sanders, Tim. *The Likeability Factor: How to Boost Your L-factor & Achieve Your Life's Dreams.* New York: Crown, 2005.

Schramm, Jennifer, Joseph Coombs, and Justina Victor. *SHRM Workplace Forecast—2011.* Alexandria: SHRM, 2011.

"A Service Economy." *America—Engaging the World.* America.gov Archive, 7 Apr. 2008, www.america.gov/st/econ-english/2008/April/20080415222038eaifas0.9101831.html.

Society for Human Resource Management and The Economist. *Global Firms in 2020—The Next Decade of Change for Organisations and Workers.* London: Rep. Economist Intelligence Unit Limited, 2010.

Wang, Jennifer, and Kara Ohngren. "The Disrupters: Forces Driving Change in 2011." *Entrepreneur,* 2 Dec. 2010, www.entrepreneur.com/article/printthis/217508.html.

We Are the First [username]. "Preparing Your Business to Go Global." *Small Business Ideas,* 22 Nov. 2010, www.wearethe1s.org/small-business/preparing-your-business-to-go-global.

About the Author

First they ignore you, then they laugh at you, then they fight you, and then YOU WIN!

– Gandhi

Pamela J. Green is a champion for HR practitioners and a living example of perseverance in the face of adversity. She often talks about her experiences in leadership and in HR during her speeches, and jokes that after she speaks, people tell her she has great stories and always want to know if they are true. Her reply, "You just can't make this stuff up! Just when I think I've experienced it all, something else happens—I'm afraid if I blink, I'll miss something!" Before going into Association Management and taking a role as Chief Membership Officer, with the Society for Human Resource Management, she served as the top HR professional in organizations such as HeadStart and the American Red Cross. With over 17 years of HR experience, she also holds both a bachelor's degree in business and human resources and a master's degree in business administration (MBA) from Franklin University in Columbus, Ohio, where she was born and raised.

Now residing in the beautiful city of Bowie, Maryland, she prefers to spend her personal time with her husband, Ray, and spirited grade school-aged son, Joshua (who lovingly believes his teacher knows more than his mom and dad). She enjoys hanging out with her family and friends both near and far. When not doing that, she prefers traveling, public speaking, writing, and just making people laugh.

As a certified Senior Professional in Human Resources (SPHR), Pamela has served the profession in many capacities, including volunteering for the United Way of Central Ohio, InRoads Columbus, and New Directions Career Center, and she currently sits on the board for the PG County Child Resource Center in Largo, Maryland, and the Executive Section Council for ASAE in Washington, DC. In addition, she is a lifetime member of the National Association of African Americans in Human Resources (NAAAHR) and the Founding President of the NAAAHR of Greater Columbus Chapter. A highly sought-after public speaker, Pam has been both facilitator and public speaker for events sponsored by the Congressional Black Caucus, American Society for Healthcare Human Resource Professionals, The Ohio State University Fisher School of Business, Biz Summits, and many major corporations. She has been quoted for by magazines and newspapers including Associations Now, Biz Summits, Columbus Post Newspaper, and many blogs and online publications.

In addition, Pam travels throughout the country annually speaking to audiences where attendance can be several hundred to several thousand on topics such as strategic business, human resources, leadership, and career development topics to name a few. In November 2006, she was honored when the Greater Columbus Chapter announced that their new annual HR Leadership Award was being named the Pamela J. Green HR Leadership Award!

Connect with Pam on Twitter, LinkedIn, and SHRM Connect, or visit her in the Green Room at **www.pamelajgreen.com.**

CPSIA information can be obtained at www.ICGtesting.com
Printed in the USA
LVOW12s0030080714

393314LV00018BA/283/P